institute of financial services

Customer Relationship Management

Neil Russell-Jones

Institute of Financial Services
IFS House
4-9 Burgate Lane
Canterbury
Kent
CT1 2XJ

T   01227 818649
F   01227 479641
E   editorial@ifslearning.com

Institute of Financial Services publications are published by The Chartered Institute of Bankers, a non-profit making registered educational charity.

Typeset by Kevin O'Connor

Printed by Antony Rowe Ltd, Wiltshire

© The Chartered Institute of Bankers 2002

Reprinted 2004

ISBN 0-85297-609-7

Contents

Contents

I

FOUNDATIONS

1

INTRODUCTION

Topics in this chapter

- About this book
- Objectives
- Structure
- How to use the book

1.1   About this book

This book is about Customer Relationship Management. It looks at all aspects of the topic from the initial concept phase, through developing and planning the initiative and on to implementation of a Customer Relationship Management initiative.

It is not about systems but about real practical organizational and customer-focused issues that face organizations and their personnel when considering such a programme.

1.2   Objectives of the book

This book has been written with two objectives in mind.

Firstly: to serve as a textbook for the **Institute of Financial Services**. It covers part of the Diploma in Financial Services Management – specifically the **Customer Relationship Management (CRM)** module. Each chapter denotes which parts of the syllabus it covers and the main topics therein.

Note, however, that some chapters cover more than one part of the syllabus; and equally some parts are covered in more than one chapter.

Secondly: it has been written to serve as an introduction to Customer Relationship Management and as a readable and useful book for students of the subject generally or interested readers. It is therefore structured in the logical sequence for:

- understanding and establishing a Customer Relationship Management programme;
- developing a Customer Relationship Management programme;

- information gathering; and then
- implementing Customer Relationship Management.

1.3   Structure

To meet these objectives the book is divided into three parts:

The first section – **Foundations** – lays the foundations for an understanding of Customer Relationship Management. This covers the definition of Customer Relationship Management, the development of Customer Relationship Management, the application of Customer Relationship Management in financial services and the implications for an organization if it seeks to implement a Customer Relationship Management initiative. It concludes with an analysis of why so many Customer Relationship Management initiatives fail.

The second section – **Developing a Customer Relationship Management initiative** – explores the steps necessary to establish a Customer Relationship Management initiative. It focuses on understanding your customers, how to collect information about your customers (and competitors) and then how to use that information and that understanding to build relationships with your customers. It then explores the role of IT in a Customer Relationship Management initiative and finally concludes by examining how to develop a Customer Relationship Management strategy and what that means.

The final section – **Making it happen** – focuses on the practical implications and usage of a Customer Relationship Management initiative. Key aspects include planning the programme; implementing the programme; changing behaviours and culture to maximize from a Customer Relationship Management initiative and why it is necessary to monitor it and to keep developing it.

At the end of the book is a glossary of terms, an index and other useful items.

1.4   How to use the book

Each chapter contains the following items:

- a summary of the contents;
- what you should be able to understand at the end of the chapter;
- further reading on the subject (as relevant).

Some definitions

Throughout this book there are some terms that are used frequently. A full glossary can be found in the appendices. For avoidance of confusion you should note the following:

any reference to him or her includes both genders and often the plural.

Other terms include:

- **Buyers**

  Those people, groups of people or organizations that purchase the offerings made in a market. Sometimes referred to as clients or customers and sometimes called consumers. Note however that not all buyers are end consumers of the offering and may include warehouses, re-sellers' agents and retailers. Manufacturers often buy raw materials and finished goods.

- **Sellers**

  Those people groups of people and organizations that offer a product or service to the market and attempt to meet needs and wants and to match demand with supply.

Without both buyers and sellers there is no market.

- **Market**

  The mechanism whereby buyers and sellers are brought together. This may be a physical location – eg Lloyds of London or a stock exchange or just the intangible set of transactions that effect buying and selling – eg the London Foreign Exchange (F/X) market which is just a collection of telephone lines and limits in banks, brokers and other players. Within a market there can be many sub-markets. For example in financial services you could split it into banking, insurance, asset management, securities, treasury and other services. In turn banking could be split into retail banking, wholesale, international, corporate, institutional, and investment and merchant banking. Similarly insurance includes personal lines, re-insurance, marine, life, energy, special risks, and so on. These splits are of course not set in stone, and, with the blurring of boundaries driven by change, often overlap – eg bancassurance, allfinanz, etc.

- **Product**

  A manufactured item such as a tank, a CD player, a bottle of whisky or a four-wheel drive car – where there is a *physical* delivery (or the opportunity for it, which might not be exercised).

- **Service**

  The supply of people-based services – eg professional advice, architecture, dry cleaning; or intangible items such as an overdraft or insurance or IT management of systems through facilities management.

Products and services are used to mean both.

- **Brand**

  The actual name that items are sold or marketed under:

  - Galaxy, Dairy Milk, Bourneville plain, Milky Bar are all types of chocolate

  - Boddingtons, Carling, Guinness, Dos Equis are all types of beer

  - Barclays, HSBC, Nationwide, Abbey National, Royal Bank of Scotland, Coutts (even though a part of the latter) are all banks of one type or another

- CGNU, Prudential, Swiss Re, Scottish Widows, Jardines, Willis Coroon are all types of insurance company

- Visa, Mastercard, American Express and Diners are all charge or credit cards.

2

WHAT IS CUSTOMER RELATIONSHIP MANAGEMENT?

Topics in this chapter

- What is Customer Relationship Management – definition and concepts
- What it is not
- Why it is important and different from other initiatives
- Customer Value Propositions

Syllabus topics covered

- What is Customer Relationship Management: Definition and Concepts.

Introduction

Customer Relationship Management is not a new concept. It has been around for many years and in the beginning banking was founded wholly within this concept. In the last 30 years or so the concept was eclipsed by many other things and events and much of the customer focus was lost as organizations were preoccupied with mergers, recession, new technologies and regulation. Recently however it has been rediscovered as a major tenet of customer retention – driven by the increasing complexity of the market, increasing competition and by several studies that have highlighted the benefits of customer management.

One of the key precepts underpinning a supplier:buyer relationship (and customers are buyers and financial services organizations are suppliers) is that as a supplier you have no right to expect that they will continue to take your offerings. You have to **earn that right** and keep on demonstrating that you are still 'worthy' to supply them.

It is important also to understand that acquisition of customers is not the same as retention. There are different drivers or factors that influence customers in each case, as shown below. Acquisition is necessary to build share initially – it is the first relationship that they have with you. This establishes a 'bridgehead' of good faith upon which you must build to keep them and further develop the relationship – Retention.

Figure 1: Acquisition and retention have different drivers

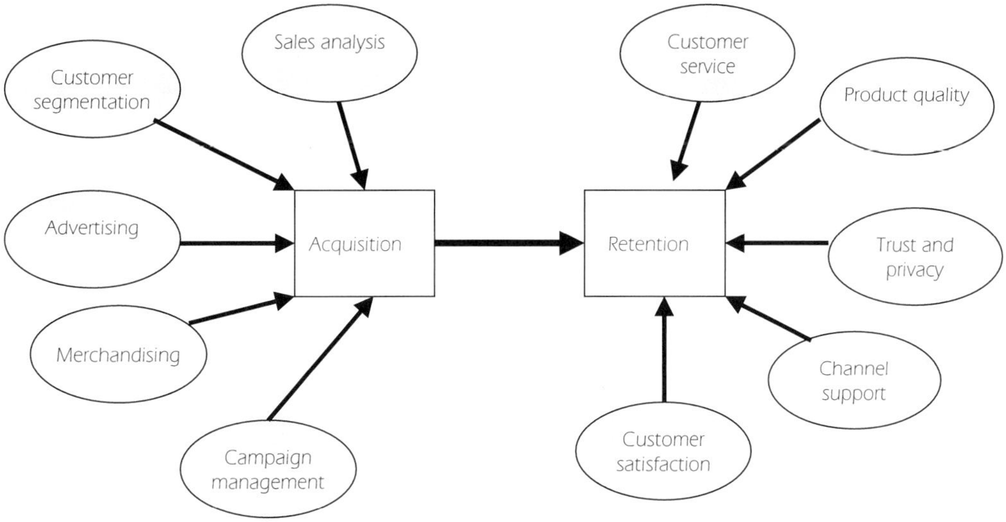

The critical factors here are satisfaction and trust – satisfaction with the service and trust in the organization and its staff. NB – you can only retain customers after you have acquired them. Customer Relationship Management is the mechanism for retaining customers.

2.1 Customer Relationship Management – definition

Customer Relationship Management can be defined as the use of a wide range of techniques including:

- marketing
- research
- communication
- service tailoring
- pricing

To allow you to:

- understand who is your customer
- isolate the 'best' customers (those with whom you desire to have long-standing relationships)
- create relationships stretching over time and involving multi-interactions

- manage that relationship to mutual advantage

- seek to acquire more of those 'best' customers

This applies equally to personal (retail) and corporate customers.

As the model shows it is about taking several inputs:

- customer base

- products

- competition

- staff

- strategy

… and synthesizing them via the Customer Relationship Management programme and creating outputs that improve your return from your customers. Other factors are regulation, your systems that support the initiative and your culture.

Figure 2: CRM – the model

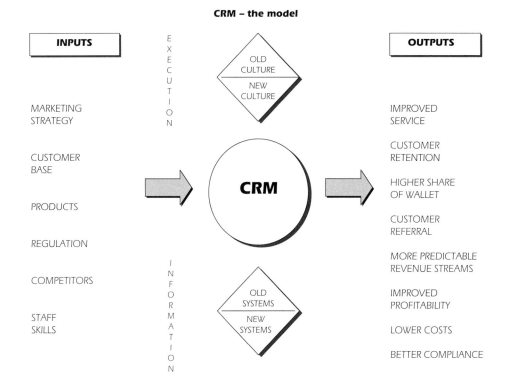

Marketers refer to how customers are viewed and the 'strategies' that cover them as 'offensive' and 'defensive'. Offensive is concerned with acquiring new customers, which is important if a business is to grow. Nevertheless you must not forget your existing customer base, because no matter how many new customers you attract, you cannot grow if your existing base is continually being eroded.

Therefore, you need to consider both – defensive marketing looks at the existing customer base and Customer Relationship Management sets the ground rules and lays the foundations for defensive marketing upon which you can subsequently build for offensive marketing – winning new customers.

2.2 Why is it being used?

In many respects it is nothing new – many years ago retailing of anything (groceries, fruit, clothes, banking) was very personal. The people providing the services/products would know their customers intimately, their special requirements, their family special occasions etc. So a bank manager in, say, Gurneys Bank in East Anglia or Drummonds Bank in Scotland in the early 19th Century would know his customers' needs and tailor his services and his decisions to match individual needs. Banks would be 'family bankers' to generations.

As economic requirements changed and different pressures were exerted on banks (and other industries), including the need or desire to merge coupled with changes in distribution, so this intimacy was eroded. The recent changes to technology, enabling so much more, when linked to the changes in legislation covering financial services, have meant that distribution channels are now much more complex than they used to be. Customers can now contact you not only in person (face to face) but also remotely.

Face to face can take several forms including:

- In the branch – where the customer calls in to see someone – with or without an appointment

- Personal visits at home – either by personal bankers or by a sales force – eg 'Men from the Pru'

- Work place visits – where many people are seen in one go – such as pension consultants visiting a factory to discuss issues relating to a company scheme

- In-shop stalls – where space in other outlets is taken and used to 'sell' services

- Via third party agencies – where others meet clients on your behalf – eg mortgage brokers who seek deals and then pass them onto deliverers

Figure 3: Distribution channels are much more complex

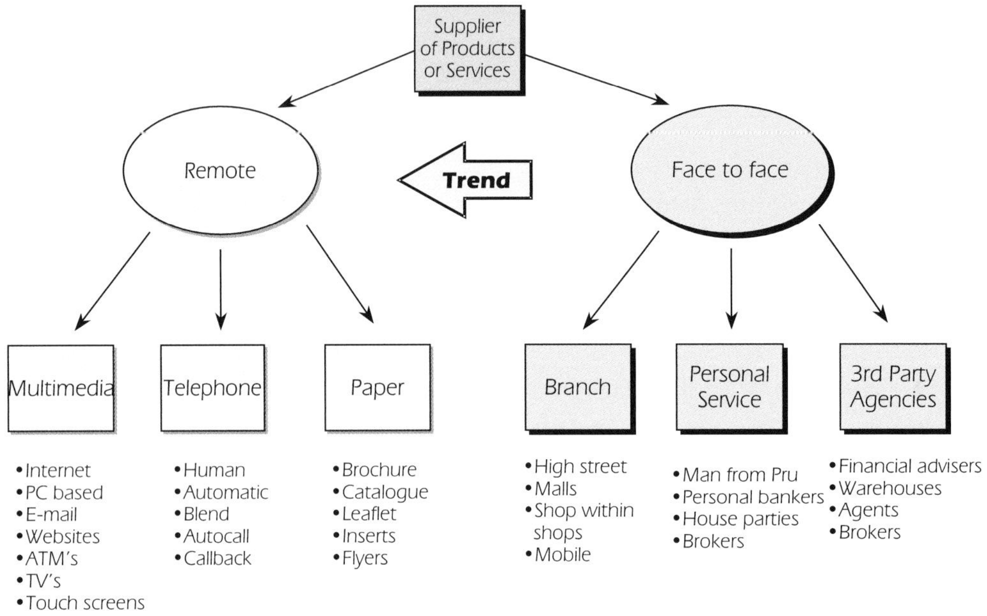

```
                    ┌──────────┐
                    │ Supplier │
                    │of Products│
                    │or Services│
                    └──────────┘
            ┌───────────┘    └───────────┐
      ╭──────────╮    ◁═══════    ╭──────────╮
      │  Remote  │     Trend       │Face to face│
      ╰──────────╯                 ╰──────────╯
```

Multimedia	Telephone	Paper	Branch	Personal Service	3rd Party Agencies
•Internet	•Human	•Brochure	•High street	•Man from Pru	•Financial advisers
•PC based	•Automatic	•Catalogue	•Malls	•Personal bankers	•Warehouses
•E-mail	•Blend	•Leaflet	•Shop within shops	•House parties	•Agents
•Websites	•Autocall	•Inserts	•Mobile	•Brokers	•Brokers
•ATM's	•Callback	•Flyers			
•TV's					
•Touch screens					

Channels can be remote or face to face

Recently there has been a major increase in the use of remote channels supported by step changes in technology coupled with increasing awareness and lower costs. While this has some great advantages for both users and suppliers – especially for new entrants who can establish distribution mechanisms at much lower costs due to an absence of bricks and mortar using 'greenfield' sites, eg Egg, First Direct, Cahoot, Direct Line and so on – it has greater implications for suppliers as the type of contact has changed and, therefore, the opportunities for discussion and relationship building, and understanding of needs are no longer there or have changed radically. As a result, in order to capitalize on the new channels, and to identify and exploit opportunities, different ways of dealing with customers are required and this has serious implications for staff and organizations etc that are explored subsequently.

Major types of remote channels are:

● **Paper** – has been in use for years without really being considered as remote. For example many organizations sell through catalogues – Grattons, GUS, John Norris – and some wholly so. Also many organizations use their connections with customers to send advertising information to them – some well considered and targeted, much of it 'junk';

● **Telephone** – at its basic level it was a method for customers to contact their suppliers and discuss issues or make appointments. It really took off, however, in the 80s and 90s with the establishment of call centres dedicated to telephone usage – the best known example of this was Direct Line which was a ground breaker in insurance terms. It required, however, a deep understanding of the true implications. Some organizations merely put people in a room with telephones and called that a call centre. However, a true call centre is something wholly different with different ethos, culture and modus operandi from usual business. It requires different scripts, different training and usually different products.

Recent advances in mobile telephone technology have given an extra fillip to this channel and it looks set for another major advance as banking on the move becomes a real possibility.

- **ATMs** – initially used to take pressure off cashiers and although basically just cash dispensers they have now metamorphosed into virtual offices and you can carry out many transactions via this channel;

- **Touch screen** – a method of transacting business without a human interface;

- **PC** – pioneered many years ago but lacked the basic infrastructure and understanding and only came into its own in the 90s – again driven by greater penetration and reducing costs of technology. It is now generally accepted although usage is low but growing – in the USA 'social deprivation' is often taken to mean no access to the Internet/PCs. As technology advances – eg GPS-based which allows access to servers remotely without dialling-up, this channel will also increase dramatically in usage;

- **e-mail/Internet** – exploded in recent years and facilitates PC usage. Has given rise to a whole new industry focusing on 'e' but it took a serious knock in 2001 when the **'South Sea Bubble dot.com'** finally burst and the market took a healthy dose of realism. Remains the fastest growing channel and will no doubt replace much of the business transacted through other media;

- **Interactive Television** – linked to the Internet but uses your home TV instead of PCs. Originally pioneered many years ago in the 70's but the support, infrastructure and functionality was not there, and this channel required another 20 years to start gaining real acceptance.

2.3 Where Customer Relationship Management fits in with this

As a result of these changes organizations need to change their operating procedures enormously to ensure that they can capitalize on the changed opportunities and contact types.

Customer Relationship Management is the mechanism for this.

With the advent of mergers; multi-products; centralization of decisions; multi-channel access; automated transaction processing etc, managers rarely see their customers, never mind get to know them. Often they are not even involved in many of the decisions. As a result the impersonal service leads to a feeling of estrangement and clients become 'orphans' (and, therefore, prey to offers from competitors) and loyalty is greatly reduced. A good example of this is the mortgage market where the average life of a mortgage has fallen from ten through seven to around three years. This has implications for many of the products sold because the profit is based around a greater longevity of mortgages which only start to make money in subsequent years.

Customer Relationship Management is a mechanism to bring back that understanding and empathy.

Case study: Nationwide's CRM experience

The magic acronym 'CRM' (customer relationship management) in all its different guises has been much written about as the amicable solution to the financial services industry's love/hate relationship with its customers. Nationwide, in line with its mutual status, lays great store in what it calls 'the member's experience' – in other words, how the customer deals with the society either through its staff or the delivery channels it offers.

One of the fastest growing delivery channels in terms of customer usage for financial organizations is, of course, the Internet. Nationwide's website banking service has about 1,500 new e-bankers per day and 900,000 registered users. In September 2001 alone the site was visited 2.4m times and each month about 60,000 e-contacts or e-enquiries are dealt with by the Society's internet contact team.

Automation is the answer

In order to cope with this volume of enquiries, a CRM system has been installed that partly automates electronic responses back to the customer. Senior operations manager Mark Cromack says: 'The "auto-suggest" system's response to customer enquiries is one area where automation is ideally suited to cut costs and enhance a user's experience of the site.'

About 60% of enquiries are dealt in this way, sorting out simple questions such as those relating to technical issues. For Internet queries that require an operator's input, the system is designed so a member of the team can personalize and craft an appropriate response before replying.

This automation has resulted in a 25% reduction in the Society's average e-mail response-handling time of six minutes (eight minutes for a secure e-mail, which might contain sensitive details such as account information). It has helped the team exceed its service level target for five consecutive months of replying to 90% of e-mails within 24 hours of a customer query being sent.

Good deal going

The system's effect on that other three-letter acronym ROI (return on investment) has also been positive – halving the average cost per customer contact across the board from £4 to £2. (The average call centre operational cost per contact is £1.80.)

There has also been a good ROI in terms of staff retention. Cromack comments: 'The Internet contact team of about 50 people has a staff turnover of about 4%. This compares favourably with average call centre staff turnover which is conservatively put at 8%.'

The staff in the Internet team are recruited from the call centre staff in order to build on existing knowledge of the products and services available to customers. Research by Nationwide has also shown that the part automation of the contact process has actually led to very positive human feedback, with one in 200 contacts generating a compliment from customers. Over 15% of these single out an adviser for praise – probably the single most important factor in making the contact centre staff feel motivated and valued in an often-maligned role.

Nationwide is now looking at further enhancements to the system, including implementing a natural language processing product, which will be able to understand customers' questions as if they were ordinary e-mails. It will also be able to respond to customer enquiries in real-time, giving them the option to enter into a live chat with a contact centre adviser or direct them straight to the most relevant part of the website in order to answer their query. It is expected that this could become available to users of Nationwide's website by early 2002.

CRM systems are often mooted as tools to sort the wheat from the chaff, giving financial services companies the opportunity to retain and reward their most valuable customers at the expense of others less valued. However, it is a suggestion that Cromack vehemently rejects as a tactic used by Nationwide: 'Some banks might use this "Gold Card" approach of using CRM systems to prioritise customers. It's not a policy we follow at Nationwide.'

2.4 What Customer Relationship Management is about

Customer Relationship Management is about enhancing customer service, sales effectiveness and marketing strategy both to maintain the relationship with the customer over a longer period as well as to gain a greater share of your customer's wallet (or spend). It is usually supported by an integrated information system, which is used to plan, schedule and control the pre- and post-sales activities in an organization.

The objectives of implementing such a programme are to create and sustain a **customer-driven culture** by focusing on the total customer experience. This enables you to:

● identify;

● build stronger relationships with; and

● retain;

the best customers.

It will also allow you to attract new profitable customers. This requires organizational alignment that delivers exceptional customer value that delights your customers – efficiently and profitably. This latter point is important, as making profit is key to the concept of Customer Relationship Management. It is about changing the way you regard your customers and the way that your organization interacts with them in order to deliver better, more focused services in return for which the customers use more of your services, more frequently in order for you to make money. Make no mistake: increased profit is the key reason for initiating Customer Relationship Management.

Why is this important?

Much research has been carried out into the nature of sales and service and a few paradigms have emerged:

- attention to clients is often ex-post rather than ex-ante – ie when something goes wrong (often too late) ;

- cross-selling is more cost-effective (product penetration) and income/profit streams are more predictable;

- development costs are amortized across a longer period therefore margins are better;

- it is much more expensive to acquire new customers because acquisition has an inherent cost:

  - marketing and sales to a new 'universe' of clients;

  - new account set-up costs;

  - low initial levels of transactions;

  - discounts and offers to attract them in;

  - as they have no established relationship upon which to build they are less likely to give you the benefit of the doubt and more likely to leave;

- there is a high correlation between retention and profitability and retained customers are much better in the long run because:

  - they buy more;

  - they pay more;

  - they cost less to serve;

- customers are more likely to stay with you the longer they have been with you. (NB Many organizations, however, misread the fact that customers have stayed with them for a long time for loyalty – when in many cases their was no other choice or customers were not aware of the options – and accordingly as their service deteriorated or competitors entered the market with attractive propositions, they paid the price when customers went elsewhere);

Figure 4: Relationship management – objectives

Move a 'suspect' to a 'partner'

- suspect   may have a need
- prospect   may do business with you
- customer   has done business with you once
- client   has a longer-term business relationship with but may be neutral or even negative
- supporter   likes the firm but supports you passively
- advocate   supports overtly – does your marketing for yo
- partner   is in full partnership with you

General sales cycle   CRM areas of focus

- long-standing customers move from being 'customers' to being 'partners', ie they:
  - bring an increasing share of transactions to you;
  - they bring others in their 'family' (business or personal) to you;
  - they become advocates of your services;
  - they 'sell' on your behalf.

Relationship marketing is about a continuous dialogue with the best customers, learning and working together. It is based on exploiting the potential of customer databases to understand customers better; to target and tailor solutions; and working with customers to find new, innovate products and services ... and also recruiting new customers.

The aim of Customer Relationship Management is to encourage better behaviour by, for example, putting focus on service benefits, or by segmenting benefits in some way to target requirements more effectively.

Case Study: BA Executive Club

BA runs an Executive Club with three levels of membership (Blue, Silver and Gold) with different benefits at each level – silver and gold allow you access to BA lounges around the world, and priority bookings whereas blue does not and is the basic entry level. The levels reflect the flights and spending that are made with BA. More 'points' are awarded in premium cabins and on longer flights and on premium routes. There is also a scheme for awarding airmiles, which are separate from the Executive club points and allow you to redeem them against flights. BA collects information on members and collates it into its database. This includes knowledge of flying patterns and they also ask members what they would like to see and receive as members. They then use this information to target members with special offers and to provide information that they think will be relevant.

Customer Relationship Management is, then, about harnessing the knowledge you hold within your database, cross-correlated with external sources of information that are relevant, to personalize service, target promotions, cross-sell other products and increase customer loyalty.

2.5   What it is not

There is much literature around on Customer Relationship Management in books, magazines, position papers and articles. Virtually without exception these concentrate on two things – systems and the Internet. There are many references to *e-Customer Relationship Management* as though this was the answer or the only factor. It is not. The Internet is merely another channel – albeit one that has profound implications for customer management due to the opportunities it affords, and the influence it has on other channels and on service generally by increasing the range of choices available and facilitating comparisons – but it is just that, one channel in many.

A Customer Relationship Management programme must, of course, take the Internet and its implications into account but it is merely one aspect of the channels through which you contact and interface with your customers and by no means the most frequent or important – yet. Balance is important and understanding your organization's marketing strategy – eg channel mix – is an important factor in Customer Relationship Management.

Any Customer Relationship Management programme that concentrates solely or principally on the Internet will ultimately fail. This is because Customer Relationship Management is about gathering information from your customers through *all* channels and then using it to provide a seamless and valuable service to them to mutual advantage – again through all channels.

Similarly a lot of attention is focused on the systems and reams of paper are wasted describing the selection procedure and the relative qualities between systems and providers. Any Customer Relationship Management programme run in that fashion – ie focusing on IT and ignoring the business and customer aspects – or at least paying them insufficient attention – will also fail.

2.6   Loyalty

To increase revenue from Customer Relationship Management, the value created to you must exceed your cost of delivery. You must reward and reinforce your customers' desirable behaviours and target the best customers with the best value. You must also offer real value, which is relevant and convenient.

Because there is a cost associated with acquisition it is critical, therefore, for a financial services institution (as it is for any organization) to seek to develop very long-term relationships with customers.

Figure 5: Customer relationships are important

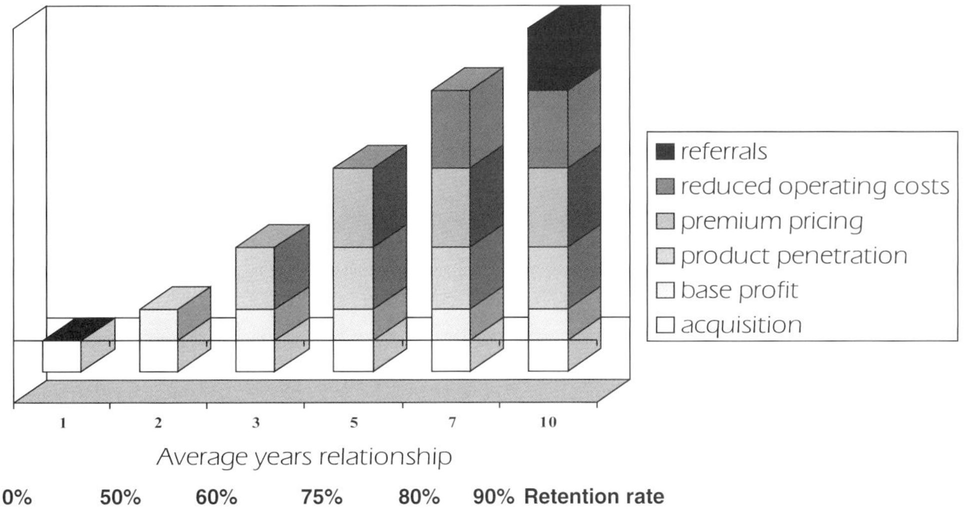

Average years relationship

| 0% | 50% | 60% | 75% | 80% | 90% Retention rate |

Source: Various

A lot of research has been undertaken into why loyal customers should be better for you. The diagram above shows why this is. It looks at the life of a relationship and looks at the cost/benefits to an organization from a longer-term relationship. The profit increases due to initial absorption of costs, increased product penetration, premium pricing opportunities, reduced operating costs and ultimately extra business from referrals (which have a lower acquisition cost than cold new customers). In addition the retention rate increases (ceteris paribus) as the relationship matures and the customer loyalty grows.

Loyalty is about the conscious decision of your customers to commit their continual repurchases to your brand. It is:

● driving an extra few miles to do your shopping

● recommending it to your best friend

● an emotional and rational 'lock-in'

● taking a suite of products or services instead of a one-off relationship

● sometimes encouraged by an incentive or reward

● a better path to profit.

Loyalty is essentially a one-way commitment for which the customer may receive a reward, but it is also about relationships, ie it is about a two-way interaction in which both sides create and exchange mutual benefit.

Figure 6: Loyalty drives business success

LOYALTY EFFECTS				BUSINESS RESULT Revenue Profit Share		
Customer Retention				35	30	27
Customer Lifetime				25	30	20
Share of Purchases				24	24	33
Recommendation				17	16	20
				100	100	100

LOYALTY DRIVERS

Delight	15	16	19	23
Satisfaction	38	37	36	48
Attractiveness	19	18	23	16
Working Together	18	18	16	8
Inertia and Barriers	10	11	6	5
	100	100	100	100

Source: EFQM 1995

Inertia does not equal loyalty!

Every company knows that customer satisfaction is important to business success, however, it is not generally realized that satisfaction itself is not the panacea that delivers increased profits and a greater share of customers' wallets. Satisfaction is only a feeling (and is accordingly ephemeral and as likely to disappear as quickly, if not more quickly, than it was generated) which contributes towards customers' behaviour, but takes no account of the effects on customers from competition. In competitive markets, with little differentiation, satisfaction of customers is not enough – customer loyalty is required to ensure business success. Loyalty must be combined with satisfaction to be effective. The table below contrasts these two areas.

Figure 7: Satisfaction v. Loyalty

Source: EFQM

Where satisfaction is high but loyalty is low the market is highly competitive and differentiation is low. Customers tend to move driven by factors such as price but they will stay if you can differentiate and build on the satisfaction.

Where loyalty is high but satisfaction is low the loyalty that they have is acting as a barrier to egress – eg where customers have a lot of capital invested in a frequent flyer scheme and do not wish to write it off by moving to another airline's. However you remain vulnerable to counter-offers by competitors.

Where satisfaction is high and loyalty is high you are doing the right things for them; your customers are delighted and are the key customers that you wish to retain.

There are several states between your customer and you – ranging from awareness through trust/transaction to satisfaction/loyalty and ultimately to advocacy. The objective of customer relationship is to move customers rapidly up through these levels and then maintain as many as possible in either the advocacy level but at least the loyalty level.

Figure 8: The relationship hierarchy

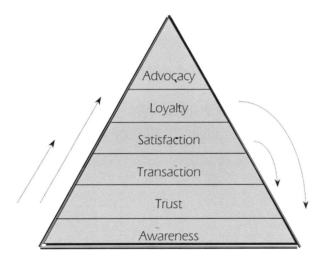

Source: MORI Excellence Model

Many organizations have introduced loyalty schemes to support this movement into the top levels. Examples of some loyalty programmes include:

- Shell SMART
- Tesco Clubcard
- Argos Premier Points
- GM Card

- Homebase Spend&Save

- Air Miles

- American Express Membership Miles

- Ede & Ravenscroft

- Boots

- Marks and Spencer

When the Marks and Spencer card was launched the publicity that it generated was phenomenal. When the analysis below was undertaken it showed that Marks and Spencer had a very high degree of advocates. Since then however Marks and Spencer has had a torrid time in the market – although with a new CEO and a new brand – 'per una' – it has made some recovery. Similarly since then Tesco has made further gains in the marketplace and overtaken Sainsburys in many people's minds. The key message here is that loyalty is not to be taken for granted.

Figure 9: Retailing relationship levels

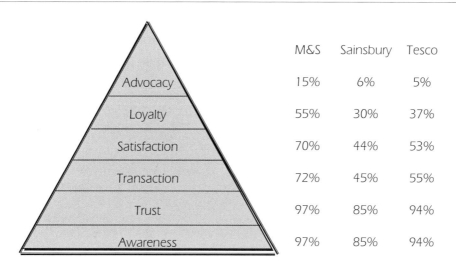

	M&S	Sainsbury	Tesco
Advocacy	15%	6%	5%
Loyalty	55%	30%	37%
Satisfaction	70%	44%	53%
Transaction	72%	45%	55%
Trust	97%	85%	94%
Awareness	97%	85%	94%

Although loyalty can be built up – it must not be taken as a given and you need to continually work on it.

Source: MORI using base of those in market for each business

2.7   Customer Value Propositions (CVP)

This term was coined in the 1980s by two American academics and consultants (Michael Lanning and Dr Lynn Phillips[1]). The thrust of the thinking behind this is that a customer

---

[1]   Michael Lanning and Dr Lynn Phillips

chooses a product or service over its competitors' products and services because it offers the greatest positive combination of end-result Benefits and Price (that is the greatest 'Value') in the perception of the customer. If this were not so then the only differentiator or mechanism for selling would be price.

All organizations offer one or more Customer Value Propositions – often combined together, and often without really knowing what it is that customers value – frequently stumbling over success by accident rather than design.

In truth, however, a customer will choose an offering because it offers the best trade-off between **price** (as perceived by them) and **benefits** (also as perceived by them). This equals the **value** that they feel that they are receiving from that combination of price and benefits as exemplified by the product/offering that they have bought.

It is not what **you** think that your customers value that counts, it is what they **actually** value that matters – and you need to ask them what it is – you must not guess, because you will be prejudiced.

The **Customer Value Proposition** can be defined as follows:

Benefit   *less*   Price   *equals*   Value

Where:

Benefit is the result of doing business with your organization (ie what the customer gains)

Price is the 'total cost' to the customer – which may not be solely in monetary terms and might include other issues such as travel, time and other things foregone.

This can be thought of as an equation where to be successful the answer must always be **positive** for the customer. In the long run it must also be **positive** for the organization as well. The customer therefore has two options:

● he will either **pay you more** than the competition because he perceives that he will receive **greater Benefits** from you than the competition (and therefore **greater Value**)

or

● he will select an offering that delivers **less benefit** but at a **lower price** (such as choosing a bank that is nearer for convenience sake even if it does not offer services that others further away might) thereby equalizing the Price/Benefits trade-off and taking **lower Value**.

NB He will not typically pay you more for less.

The use of Customer Relationship Management, then, is to enable organizations to ensure that they always offer that combination of benefits to the customer that will act as an imperative for the customers to choose their offerings. Note that this must also be done to the benefit of the organization to ensure that it is also equalizing its own Customer Value Proposition.

2.8   Differentiation

Many businesses competing in the same arena are perceived as very similar by the customer. The inevitable question is 'Why should I use you instead of 'X' or 'Y'…?' – and the financial services sector is no different in this respect. A business has to develop its own way of doing things – ie something that makes a **difference** – to the customer. In other words some thing, idea or way of doing things (service) that makes you stand out from the rest of the crowd – ie that **differentiates** you from everybody else (the competition). If you cannot find this thing (or equally cannot convince your customers of it) then you are reduced to competing only on price and that is a one-way ticket to oblivion – or bankruptcy – unless you have real cost advantage and can sustain low prices.

Selling yourself through differentiation is very effective – unfortunately however, developing that differential is very difficult. All of your competitors are also trying to do the same. In marketing this is often referred to as developing a *Unique Selling Proposition* (USP) and is a combination of factors that differentiate your product or service. It must also be remembered that a USP must be developed for each service or segment. It is products and services that compete in a marketplace *not* organizations, but this fact is often forgotten by many – including people that should know better, such as marketing personnel.

Segments have different needs and wants and selling financial services to, say, a single, 65-year-old man is different from selling to a 21-year-old, married woman and very different from selling to a business partnership, let alone a major corporate – even if they all want the same product. Neither can you presume that the competition is the same in each segment. – eg if you are selling insurance generally you will not find Saga competing for the business of 21-year-olds.

Equally it is what the offering does for the individual or organization that makes them buy – not how it is packaged. It is the *benefit* that it brings them that counts not the *features*. For example the fact that a facsimile machine can photocopy the documents and then store them in memory *(feature)* is not the main issue, it is that it saves time *(benefit)* because you do not need to wait until the document has 'gone through' and it will send the message using auto redial until it has been received.

What you offer a customer, therefore, is a medium for helping them to achieve their goals – whether personal, business or a combination of both (ie you are addressing their needs). It is vital therefore to understand this. A customer does not expressly want a loan – she wants to buy a car or a house or go on holiday – and a loan facilitates this by providing the money in one go which she can then use to pay for the product/service (need) and repay over a longer period.

It is similar with corporates – understanding the business needs of a customer enables you to frame the correct offer. Unless someone is engaged in import/export, majoring on your foreign or international service is useless and may turn them off you. Where they are deeply involved in trade with several countries, however, an offering that supports this type of business will be very much more acceptable *(ceteris paribus)*.

Key learning points

1. Customer Relationship Management is not a new concept but has recently been reinforced as greater understanding has been gained of the dynamics of customer buying and retention.

2. Customer Relationship Management is a mechanism for increasing customer loyalty and therefore both retention and product penetration, leading to much enhanced earnings for an organization.

3. Distribution channels have now changed and expanded considerably and it is necessary to make customers feel that they receive the same considerations whichever channel or channels that they use. This requires excellent information.

4. The lifetime value of a customer is considerable and must be factored into decisions as to which customers you wish to keep and which you do not.

5. Differentiation is critical and you must develop a differential for those segments which you have chosen as your targets and offer it as solutions to customer issues – the Customer Value Proposition.

Further reading

F Reichheld: *Loyalty Rules*

Kotler: *Principles of Marketing*

Peter Doyle: *Value Based Marketing*

3

THE CUSTOMER RELATIONSHIP MANAGEMENT MODEL

Topics in this chapter
- The model of Customer Relationship and its inputs
- Customer focus and service
- Segmentation
- Segment strategies
- Organization competencies

Syllabus topics covered
- What is Customer Relationship Management.
- Customer Relationship Management as part of a customer service quality strategy.
- Building relationships by adding value to customers cost effectively.

Introduction

The fundamental objective of a Customer Relationship Management programme is simple…:

> '…to increase the share of your take of your customers' wallet'

To do this you must of course give the customer increasing value to retain the relationship and maintain his feeling of benefit received. To this end the model of how it works is also simple. There are four basic components in analysing the customer/supplier interface:

- the universe of customers (current customers, prospects and suspects);
- the interfaces between your organization and the customer base (channels, subsidiaries, agencies);
- the model that supports it; and
- the feeds into the model.

The diagram below shows these four components.

Figure 10: The CRM model

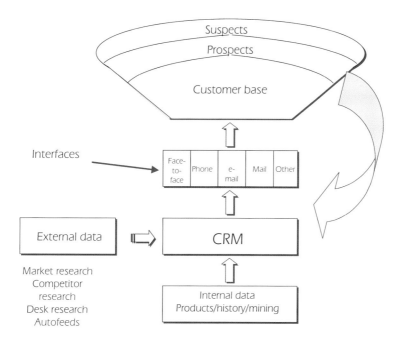

These concepts underpin the rest of the book and will be discussed in detail later.

There are some key components of Customer Relationship Management as follows:

- customer focus;
- single view/seamless service;
- proactive rather than reactive;
- segmentation by profitability;
- solutions not products;
- retention of the best (profitable) customers;
- performance-related staff remuneration;
- excellent processes supporting the services;
- having the right people with the right skills in the right place;
- continuous learning and feedback;

and these are explored over the page.

3.1   Customer focus

Historically many organizations were focused along *internal* conventions – ie account or product (usually driven by the IT system installed which allowed only this type of analysis). It was, therefore, easy to see how many current accounts you had, or how many mortgages were outstanding and which were in arrears. It was, of course, also easy to look for a particular clients' situation relative to a single product but extremely difficult in many cases to collate many disparate items that related to a customer into a single view. It was – and in many cases still is – impossible to cross-correlate products across different parts of the same group with whom a single customer has relationships. There have been some major steps in many organizations to improve this but there is still a long way to go for many.

One of the fundamental precepts and, therefore, benefits, of Customer Relationship Management is that it takes an external, customer-focused view. That is, it is able to 'cut' data along **customer lines** and provide information that relates to that customer, enabling a holistic view to be taken of the relationship in totality.

3.2   Single view/seamless service

The key elements here are data on the customer, which includes

- **standing data** – data specific to the customer;
  - *contacts* (name, address, telephone, mobile, e-mail) ;
  - *personal details* (date of birth, salary, marital and family details, hobbies, significant events);
- **relationship data** – data specific to your relationship with the customer;
  - *relationship history* (products held, relationship/account managers, cross-organizational relationships, related customers);
  - *contact history* (outbound and inbound).

This latter data must be real-time for those staff involved in interfaces with the customers (cashiers, relationship managers etc) so that they can supply a seamless service, but can be static for others (marketing etc). In the customers' eyes all members of the organization (generally) are perceived as representing the organization to the same degree and therefore each of their interactions should feel the same – allowing for differences in channels.

3.3   Proactive rather than reactive

The information held in the Customer Relationship Management database can be used to generate outputs to drive the Customer Relationship Management process and therefore allow the organization to be proactive – that is to anticipate customers' future needs and act accordingly. How much better when a customer calls in to discuss a potential mortgage or a loan for them to be told on the spot that it has been approved because (unknown to the customer) the organization has already set pre-approved limits. This gives the benefit that you are still exercising control over quality of lending – and centralizing the process – but sales-focused authority is delegated down to managers which enables them to build very strong relationships with clients by seemingly giving decisions immediately on their own authority.

Similarly for insurance, where limits, premiums and loadings, and characteristics can be pre-loaded into the life underwriting system, based on a deep understanding of the customer from the Customer Relationship Management model, which can then 'auto-accept' for most customers.

3.4   Segmentation by profitability

Segmentation is a mechanism used to divide the whole universe of customers into manageable segments. Historic marketing spoke of segmentation by all or some of the following:

- Gender
- Religion
- Race
- Nationality
- Age bands
- ACORN (A Classification Of Residential Neighbourhoods)
- Wealth/income
- Geography

However, there are difficulties with segmentation. They not only tend to embrace large 'generalizations' but also each buyer has his own needs, wants, attitudes etc and could, therefore, represent a segment of one. Clearly this would pose severe problems for marketing as everything would be personalized or individually customized.

Customization, however, need not be producing a product or service explicitly for each person but may be a modular approach based around a combination of standard or easily available products/services already in existence. This can give the feeling to a customer that he is being looked after personally while at the same time using products in existence that require no development and therefore no extra cost. It might not always be possible to reach a 100% fit – but you can usually get very close.

Case study: Travel agencies

A family of four are going on holiday and come into a travel agent to make enquiries and possibly book it. They discuss options with the agent and eventually decide what they want. The holiday is based around a set of core items:

- type of holiday

- destination

- flight times

- convenient airports

- type of hotel

- duration of holiday

- cost

...and some ancillary items such as:

- car hire

- trips

- extra services

Based on these factors a holiday is chosen. The holiday is in fact personalized to them – and it is unlikely that any other holiday makers will have exactly the same holiday. The agent will also possibly take the opportunity to sell extra services such as currency, travellers cheques or travel insurance.

Where you produce for only a few customers (eg if you are building battleships) it is relatively easy to customize for them – where you sell to larger markets it is clearly impossible. Segmentation helps to make sense of a dimorphous mass of many individuals (or companies in the corporate sector). What are traditionally recognized as segments, however, contain pitfalls for the unwary or inexperienced.

Take residential areas. Within the same post code you might have houses that have large families, small families, childless couples, several flats in the same building or even council-owned houses or sheltered accommodation and all of these would have widely differing needs and incomes and disposable levels. Any campaign targeted in this way would be a waste of time and may not generate any business at all.

Case study: Royal Bank of Scotland

Royal Bank of Scotland has several different segments at the macro level including:

- Its branch network for the majority of the customers – branded as:
  - Royal Bank of Scotland and
  - NatWest;
- Premium banking within the network of ordinary branches with special teams of premium bankers (relationship managers);
- Premium branches run on the same platform as the network, eg Drummonds;

● Coutts – a separate bank for HINWIS customers with its frock-coated bankers.

Prices for services of course vary accordingly, but customers are prepared to pay extra for the differential service – or the cachet of banking at the 'Queens' Bank' (Coutts).

If we redefine segments as 'sets of buyers who have similar needs and who respond to marketing stimuli in similar ways' we get closer to a true segment.

It is, therefore, far better to use a combination of factors – which implies very good information – and segment by **potential profitability** to the company. In fact this latter method of segmentation is the only way to make money. You must, therefore, take the following steps:

● decide on what bases you will segment;

● analyse the attractiveness of those segments for you;

● decide in which you will make money and prioritize them;

● choose the position of your offerings in those segments;

● develop your Customer Value Propositions for each.

This, therefore, implies that you must manage your customer base (segments) very carefully and get rid of those that do not make you money (or perhaps migrate them to a different service level where they can make you money). This is where the Customer Relationship Management is useful because it provides feedback on the performance of those segments and allows you to analyse them and take the right business decisions accordingly.

This may mean taking tough decisions – but it is the sign of good management that it is able to act on information and take the right actions. This enables you to ensure that you are focusing your effort in the right places – ie on those accounts or customers who will generate the best income and not on those who take too much time and yield little by way of returns.

Figure 11: Lift your game up

Building societies are often faced with these dilemmas. Many of their accounts have small balances but still require the same amount of effort as those that contain higher deposits. In addition many customers use what are in fact savings or deposit accounts as quasi-current accounts, which costs the societies money and makes them little. For them the difficulty is to maintain the balance between the perception of mutuality (cheap services to all and sundry) and profit-enhancing decisions – higher charges or closure. Good robust analysis of their accounts can assist them in understanding which customers are unprofitable and can then assist them in formulating a strategy and a plan to close the unwanted accounts and allow them to focus on the ones that make them money.

Figure 12: General segment strategies

H	Specialized, find niche 1	Aim for No1 Build on strength Eliminate weakness 2	Go for it! 3
Segment attractiveness	Minimal investment 4	Look for growth 5	Invest 6
	No-go or Exit 7	Move out 8	Milk for cash 9
L			H

CVP
strength

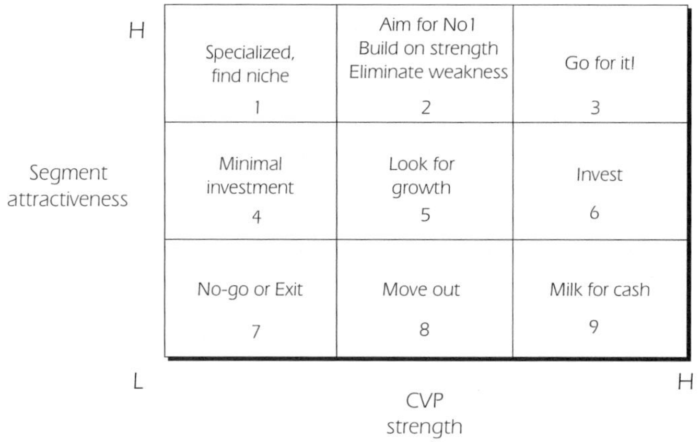

Based on the segment attractiveness and the strength of your CVP there are a
number of generic competitive strategic initiatives that can be followed

The diagram 'General segment strategies' shows some generic strategies that can be adopted after you have completed your segmentational analysis and understood the strength of your Customer Value Proposition in that segment.

They are as follows:

1. the segment is very attractive for you but your Customer Value Proposition is weak. You need to find a niche for your Customer Value Proposition and harvest market share

2. build on the strengths of the Customer Value Proposition to oust the leader – try to improve the Customer Value Proposition

3. you should easily be the market leader – nothing to stop you, but you need constantly to review your customer feedback and that your Customer Value Proposition still meets their needs so as not to lose the position

4. try to exploit the segment without spending too much, ie selling standard products without too much effort

5. you must look to grow your market share – and customer share

6. invest to gather customers based on the strength of the Customer Value Proposition which should allow you to exploit this segment

7. get out – no hope – segment unattractive and Customer Value Proposition poor – place investment elsewhere

8. begin to move out – and put investment elsewhere

9. no investment – merely sell your products based around the Customer Value Proposition to maximize return and generate cash

The key issues for consideration here are what the competitive response might be to your actions (see competitive analysis) and how easy it is to divert investment across into those segments where Customer Value Proposition is high and they are attractive.

It is worth highlighting the difference between previous segmentation and new thinking in this context:

- Traditional Segmentation (*ex ante*) – the market is segmented based on age, income, geography, type of business, etc. It is often difficult to find a relationship between these segmentation parameters and the customers' purchase decision and usage

- Needs-Based Segmentation (ex post). Because the customers' purchase decision is closely linked to the individuals' needs and preferences, customers with similar needs are grouped. When a group of customers with distinct needs and preferences is found (e.g. very little price sensitivity, and interested in new product features), common background for the group is analysed in order to operationalize this segmentation model

This then allows you to:

- choose your segments – get rid of unprofitable segments

- agree your Customer Value Propositions (CVP)

- understand your customer-shared goals

- develop customer-focused activity processes to deliver to the shared goals

- develop the 'logical roles' to carry out these processes – with the right Attributes, Skills, Knowledge (ASK)

…which is where Customer Relationship Management is focused.

3.5   Solutions not products

Many organizations are very tightly bound to their products. This is often because their development and sales are often tied to that line of thinking. As a result too often they go to a customer thinking only 'How do I sell this product or that service?'

Customers, however, do not want products or services per se. What they actually want is a solution to their problem – whatever it might be and however they define it. It is the understanding of this fact that enables a good relationship manager to put together a range of products and services that meet the needs of the customer – this 'bundling up' of products may be no more than coupling several products together – but it is the demonstration of how this bundle meets his needs and solves his problems that is critical here.

3.6 Performance-related staff remuneration

In order to use Customer Relationship Management to improve your own performance it is necessary to change the remuneration system to embed the behaviours that are required within an organization and to obviate the usually inevitable slipping back to 'what was done before'. Too often this is overlooked and although new behaviours are desired and indeed may be agreed to by staff, unless the benefits, reward and remuneration system is changed then the new behaviours will not work or will not stick. This is because people will exhibit the behaviours that they believe will reward them – even if they are counter to the desired behaviours.

3.7 Excellent processes supporting the services

Business processes are a fundamental component of any business. Efficient business processes have a major impact on the success of an organization and shape the way in which people work. In today's knowledge economy people may well be the most important assets of a company but if they have to work within the constraints of inefficient processes they cannot work effectively.

The two twin goals of processing are efficiency and effectiveness:

- Where a process maximizes efficiency it is doing what needs to be done as accurately and as fast as possible and

- Where it maximizes effectiveness it means that what is done delivers value to the customer and the organization.

(it is no good carrying out a process efficiently if it is of no value and similarly a process can be theoretically effective but if it contains inherent inefficiencies then it does not deliver when it should.)

Similarly although new technology can deliver huge benefits to a company, both in terms of cost savings and efficiency, if it is not harnessed within well-designed processes it can never achieve its full potential. Typically technology support has only **mechanized** existing processes, rather than change them to improve effectiveness and introduce real automation. This often results in extra steps in processes as people try to get round the system, to do what was done before – even where the system contains the opportunity for a step to be automated or renders it unnecessary – which usually make things worse. Real attention is needed to yield real benefits.

A good example of a poor process in most organizations is the sales process where, typically, most of the effort is expended prior to the decision. Take a typical bank process for new customers:

- identify prospects;
- develop relationships;
- find loan opportunities;
- perform analysis;
- propose loan;
- credit decision;
- **yes**:
    - underwrite deal;
    - prepare documentation;
    - close deal;
- **no**:
    - turn down.

Such processes are usually insufficiently focused, the tasks to achieve sales goals are not carried out well, and the emphasis is on new business 'hunting' rather than 'farming' the existing client base. In addition cross-disciplinary efforts are usually poor and the organizations' talents underutilized.

By moving the focus of effort to the **decision** more effective usage of time can be made – eg by pre-approving decisions, or by delegating greater authority down to managers etc or by automating the process to be one-stop capture of data and auto-acceptance. Key steps to improve processes include:

- ascertaining the time value of activities;
- mapping the processes and then changing them to drive out the inefficiencies;
- ensure that MIS provides the right data at the right time;
- strip out non-value added activities;
- streamline the processes to reduce wasted effort;
- move to self-managing teams.

and benefits would, therefore, include:

- faster throughput;

- better quality (fewer errors);
- focused marketing efforts;
- increased profit;
- improved customer satisfaction.

3.8 The right people with the right skills in the right place

You may have the best Customer Relationship Management programme in the world but if you do not have the right people then it will not help you in retaining the customers. The diagram below shows four possible scenarios:

a) where people are poor and the Customer Relationship Management is good – although the data is available customers are not treated correctly – or more likely not managed properly and quickly become dissatisfied

b) where Customer Relationship Management is poor and the people are good and the people can 'get round' the system shortcomings and still provide good service to the customer, but this is sub-optimal and not capitalizing on the investment

c) where both are poor and you will lose your best customers rapidly and end up with fewer, worse customers

d) where both are good and your customers are delighted

Clearly d) is the scenario at which to aim.

Figure 13: Customer satisfaction

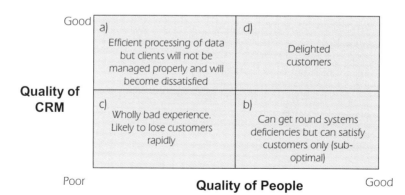

You must have both CRM Systems **and** People right to satisfy your customers, but at the right price to sell and make a profit

The best managers and staff:

- understand product width;
- have in-depth understanding of more than one product;
- know clients inside out;
- know whom to speak to internally;
- offer **value** to the client.

3.9 Continuous learning and feedback

Markets are not static – in fact the pace and scale of change seems to be increasing. It is, therefore, imperative that you keep up with what the market requires.

Failure to so this can be devastating:

'The web – it's not going to be that profound' *(Steve Jobs, Apple 1996)*

'We don't like their sound and guitar music is on its way out' *(Decca Recording [after rejecting the Beatles] 1962)*

It is useful to contrast market movements with the metamorphosis of organizational competencies.

In the example below the organization currently has its competencies fully aligned with the market expectations – ie as time has moved on the market has moved from (historical) 'old-fashioned personal banking' to (recent past) 'bricks and mortar networks' while current requirements are telesales – and the organization has continued to keep pace with the market demands.

Accordingly it is aligned with the wants ands needs of the market for delivery and can hold or even increase its market share because it is perceived to be responding to those demands.

Figure 14: How organizational competencies metamorphose

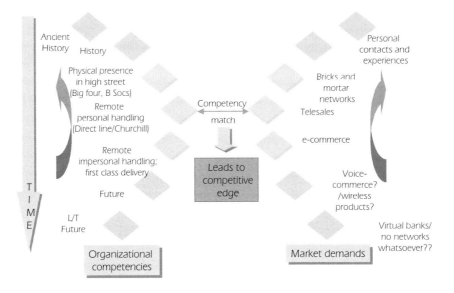

As a result the investment in the organizational competencies is yielding value to the organization. Where the competencies are out of sync with the market demands, however, it starts to lose share as customers who want a different set of competencies to fulfil their needs turn to newer or alternative players.

In the following example, therefore, the organization has allowed its organizational competencies to slip behind the market demands and there is a competency mis-match. As a result its competitors – who have changed their organizational competencies – are stealing its market share and customers because it can no longer meet the needs of its customers.

Obviously it will not be all customers who require the changes, but the trend will be well defined and an organization needs to respond to them in a measured and well thought through manner.

Figure 15: How organizational competencies metamorphose (Example for retail finance services)

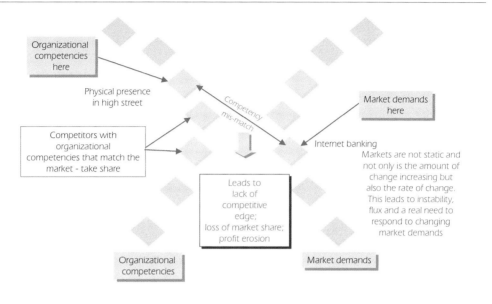

A well-run Customer Relationship Management programme will greatly facilitate this by providing feedback in a timely and critiqued fashion that will inform about decisions and lead to action in good time. This will enable strategic decisions to be taken as to how, when and where to change the organizational competencies in order that you still keep on meeting the market expectations.

It is important that you keep looking at the next but one possible development as some changes can take some time to develop, assess and then implement and may require investment. Where systems are involved (virtually in every case nowadays) this also impacts on timings and you must remember that decisions taken about IT can affect what you do for years to come.

Key learning points

1. The fundamental objective of a Customer Relationship Management programme is simply to increase the share of your take of your customers' wallet.

2. The only way of segmenting is by potential profitability – there is little point in entering a segment unless it will provide you with significant profit.

3. You must manage your customer base (segments) very carefully and get rid of those that do not make you money (or perhaps migrate them to a different service level where they can make you money).

4. Customers, however, do not want products or services per se. What they actually want is a solution to their problem – whatever it might be and however they define it. Customer Relationship Management is one of the key mechanisms for meeting understanding their problems and subsequently their needs.

5. It is necessary to keep refining your Customer Value Proposition and improving your organizational competencies to keep abreast of changes.

Further reading

Ridderstrale & Nordstrom: *Funky Business*

Shiv Mathur & Alfred Kenyon: *Creating Value* (part II)

4

WHERE CUSTOMER RELATIONSHIP MANAGEMENT FITS IN WITH STRATEGY

Topics in this chapter

- Corporate v. Competitive strategy – where Customer Relationship Management fits in
- Owning the customer
- Customer expectations and the response

Syllabus topics covered

- The importance of effective Customer Relationship Management strategies as an integral part of effective financial services marketing strategies for retail and business customers.
- Customer Relationship Management as part of a customer service quality strategy.
- The role of Customer Relationship Management in business strategy.
- Measuring performance of Customer Relationship Management.

Introduction

Many organizations – despite press announcements and brave statements in their annual report to the contrary – do not have a clearly defined vision and strategy. This is often why they seem to lack direction and do not achieve. Usually this is because the senior management does not itself have a clear vision and also do not really understand the main components of a strategy and the differences between them. As a result, therefore, senior management finds it impossible to articulate clearly, concisely and precisely what it is about. Often the board disagrees on some or all of the components and this too causes confusion.

It is important, however, that Customer Relationship Management supports whatever strategy the organization has – although sometimes it might be necessary to re-visit the strategy subtly in order to clarify the objectives and goals.

Figure 16: What a strategy does

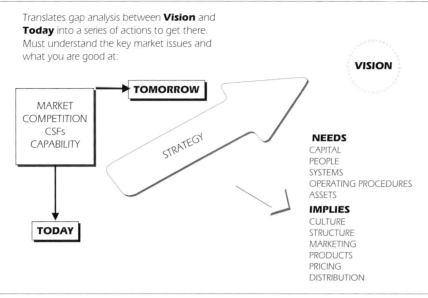

Translates gap analysis between **Vision** and **Today** into a series of actions to get there. Must understand the key market issues and what you are good at:

4.1   What is a strategy?

A strategy takes the **Vision** of an organization and develops it into a framework and subsequently translates it into a set of actions, ie steps for achieving the vision (or at least in attempting that). This will revolve around creating and then sustaining/increasing value (equity). To this end it:

- sets long-term objectives;

- drives actions;

- gives resource allocation priorities;

- defines the competency domain of the organization;

- leads to core competency development through:

    - competitive strategies;

    - functional policies;

- is simple to grasp;

- is flexible enough to respond to force majeure but changes must be defined, discussed, definitely agreed not drifted into (known as D^3);

- is viable.

Also in general a strategy:

- is deliberate – not accidental;

- is forward looking – you cannot manage the past;

- is about stakeholder satisfaction;

- tends to be all-embracing;

- deals with the 'organization as a whole' at the macro level – not the 'whole organization' (eg communist states' 'five-year plans' that tried to plan for everything down to the lowest level of granularity – which is impossible and so they always failed);

- is the articulation of the Vision, in so far as it is possible, in a way that can be understood;

- sets goals that can be measured.

There can only be one Corporate strategy, but there can be, and often are, several Competitive strategies, depending on the constituent parts of the organization. This is important in the context of Customer Relationship Management because this must reflect the competitive strategies – as developed for each segment.

4.2 Customer Relationship Management alignment with strategy

Customer Relationship Management can be effective only where it is wholly aligned with the strategy of an organization. The strategy must therefore clearly set out vision, goals and targets to provide the strategic framework for any Customer Relationship Management initiative. Without this, there is a high probability that it could fail, pull in the wrong directions or run counter to the strategic objectives.

It is important to understand the difference between the **Corporate strategy** and a **Competitive strategy**.

The **Corporate strategy** sets out the general direction for an organization as a whole (but not for the whole organization), whereas a **Competitive strategy** is based around markets and service and products.

Many organizations do not understand this vital difference and therefore their strategies are wholly inappropriate or impossible to implement effectively. The table below demonstrates the difference between these two areas and shows the different emphasis. Customer Relationship Management fits within the competitive strategy aspects.

Figure 17: Corporate v. Competitive strategy

There are key differences between these as shown below:

	CORPORATE STRATEGY	COMPETITIVE STRATEGY
OVERARCHING STATEMENT	Vision	Mission
LEVEL	Top – broadest view. Looks out; up; down; and across Sets general goals	Management level Focuses on markets Sets specific goals and targets
RESOURCES	Sets priorities	Allocates
PRODUCTS	Relates to them in a general sense. May own corporate brand	At the heart of the strategy Owns specific product brands

Most thinking and analysis focuses on **Competitive** strategy as this delivers to the **Corporate** strategy. Functional policies support these.

There are some basic questions that a competitive strategy must answer:

● what does the market want?

● what are we going to offer?

● how are we going to offer it?

● at what do we need to excel to succeed?

● how will the competition respond?

● can we make money?

● what are the internal implications?

● what do we need to change?

● will we satisfy our stakeholders?

● what are the risks and how shall we manage them?

For financial institutions it is sometimes difficult to see the clear distinction between these two because many institutions operate with mixed distribution channels. Often branches seek to service all customers and the distinctions between channels, products and customer types become blurred.

Time affects the strategy of an organization and different aspects of the whole process relate to different time frames. The vision looks very far out into the future, a corporate strategy looks at five to ten years; the competitive strategies and functional policies should be looking at three to five years whereas plans and budgets tend to be annual items.

It is important that the functional aspects of an organization (HR, IT, finance etc) produce functional policies that support the strategy moving forward. The diagram below shows the different time frames of corporate strategy, competitive strategy, functional policies and planning. As the time frame extends the items tend to become increasingly abstract. The vision is virtually 'unattainable' but serves to stretch and inspire the organization.

Figure 18: Corporate time horizons

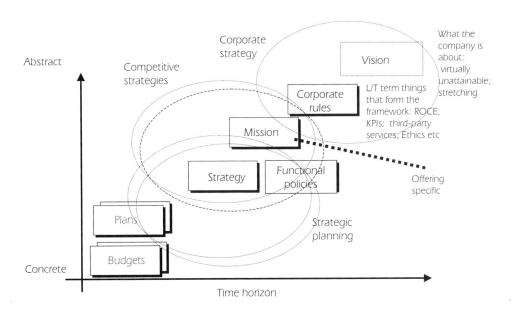

Many banks have moved to a different structural model where they have 'corporate' and 'personal' branches in an attempt to offer differentiated and focused services to their client base. This is of course laudable but it often loses some of the key customer connections. The staff of a corporate branch may, therefore, be housed in one location – or sometimes many locations – separate from the personal aspects of a customer and the connections may be lost.

Customer Relationship Management of course seeks to mend this broken channel of communication and ensure that a holistic view is taken, rather than a fragmented, individual approach based on branches.

4.3   Owning the customer

This is a big question – who exactly does own the customer?

The answer in many cases is not clear – is it the:

- branch?

- regional/local Head Office?

- mortgage manager?

- marketing department?

- relationship manager(s)?

- and so on…

Typically everyone dealing with the customer feels that they own him or her. In fact nobody 'owns' the customer – he belongs to himself. The real question is 'who controls the relationship?' – and the only answer is the organization. It can, however, and should delegate down authority for personnel to manage customers within an overall customer strategy. But to be effective it must also be within the constraints of a Customer Relationship Management programme. It is worth understanding that customers (especially corporate and 'HINWIS') increasingly *expect* their relationship to be managed.

Case Study: Software house 'X'

A software house 'X' sells several financial services products. It is global and split on product lines. This is due to an historical accident as it gained many products through corporate acquisitions. As a result it has many relationships with its larger customers in many locations across a broad range of products via several divisions/subsidiaries. As the larger clients grow more sophisticated in their purchasing they can consolidate by supplier group. This reveals that 'X' is one of their larger software suppliers in aggregate and with whom they have a large spend.

To bring them in line with internal rules and following the centralization of their IT responsibility they would like to have a 'strategic' partnership with the supplier and deal with it at a corporate, group level. Unfortunately 'X' is not structured in that way and is used to 50 relationships in 30 countries and its internal remuneration system reflects this, with local autonomy delegated down and across.

Result – a very unhappy customer who starts to review its software needs and strategy going forward – without including 'X'. Clearly 'X' needs to reorganize and establish Customer Relationship Management for its larger clients. This has great implications for its structure and culture – but failure on the other hand…

4.4   Customer expectations are changing

As competition and choice have increased new service paradigms have emerged. We are all conditioned to expect McDonald's speed of service now and we are (generally) less tolerant of delays and errors. Customers expect:

- you to know their needs and wants and in many cases to anticipate them – they have given you information over the years and expect you to use it;

- this information to be available to all staff no matter which channel they happen to be using;

- coordination across channels and distribution outlets (for some organizations internal coordination across a single channel remains an elusive goal – never mind multi-channel);

- consideration based on relationship history *not* current transactions;

- keen prices (depending on their pricing elasticity) or good value for money;

- changes of personnel to be minimal;

- few errors and instant solutions.

Case study: McDonald's[2]

Everybody knows McDonald's – it is a truly global retailer with outlets just about everywhere and is the biggest retailer in the world. It clearly gets a lot of things right – for despite the very negative comments made by many people, the outlets are always full. It clearly listens to its customers and responds and often throws in small cultural nuances to reflect local colour – eg in France in some restaurants it introduced piano players. But who knows about 'McLean' – the low-fat hamburger from McDonald's? This was introduced in response to what was felt to be a move to health-conscious eating in the USA. Product tests indicated that it tasted almost as good as the real thing. But nobody ordered it – why? – because the customer base of McDonalds is not interested in that type of product – 'McLard' is more like it – they want real burgers with chips (French Fries).

Research has shown that the most common reason for changing suppliers driven by internal factors is poor service. Often if they move location they change suppliers but that is a different driver, however if relationships are good and also coverage is available then this should also not present a problem. It is worth noting that very few are dissatisfied with the product.

---

[2] J Ridderstrale & K Nordstrom: *Funky Business* (ft.com 2000)

Figure 19: Poor customer service is driving defections

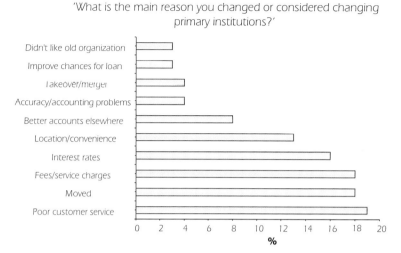

'What is the main reason you changed or considered changing primary institutions?'

Didn't like old organization
Improve chances for loan
Takeover/merger
Accuracy/accounting problems
Better accounts elsewhere
Location/convenience
Interest rates
Fees/service charges
Moved
Poor customer service

0   2   4   6   8   10   12   14   16   18   20
%

Source: ABA/Gallup Poll

The second most common reason is the price that they pay, although in many cases this is a subordinate factor to the service. If service is good and perceived as such customers will pay for it.

The next factor is convenience. Customers will trade off a lot for convenience and this does not necessarily mean having a branch within one minute's walk. It does mean that access is convenient – ie cash dispensers have changed the ability of customers to get cash out to effectively 24 hours and almost totally location independent.

It is, therefore, important to focus on the service that customers receive – and more importantly that they perceive that they receive. Customer Relationship Management is a fundamental aspect of this approach.

The following section focuses on a well-known approach to analysis of customer needs and wants and the levels of service provided – Kano analysis.

4.5   Kano analysis

Dr Noriaki Kano – a Japanese academic – has carried out extensive research into customer management as part his studies into TQM and customer management[3]. In particular he has shown that merely meeting what are supposed customer requirements – ie those at the 'surface level' – can cause serious issues if the service provider is unaware of the different – or deeper – needs/requirements.

He states that you run the danger of:

---

[3]   Kano, Noriaki: 'A perspective on quality activities in American firms' *California Management Review* Spring 1993 p12(20)

- providing superfluous quality – ie quality that is not required (price/value trade-off) (by overemphasizing high quality enabling factors – see below)

- partially delighting the customer – but failing miserably in another area resulting in lost customers (missing key 'critical' factors – see below)

- focusing on what customers say (wants) and not what they really think (needs)

The diagram graphs (in an abstract manner) **customer satisfaction** and examines two key criteria – the balance between **delight** and **dissatisfaction** and the achievement of customer requirements that you can attain by focusing on the two types of 'factors' – **enabling** (bottom right quadrant) and **critical** (top left quadrant). The vertical axis is the customers' response to your achievement of the different factors – ie how well you fulfill the customers' requirements.

Figure 20: Types of requirement (Kano diagram)

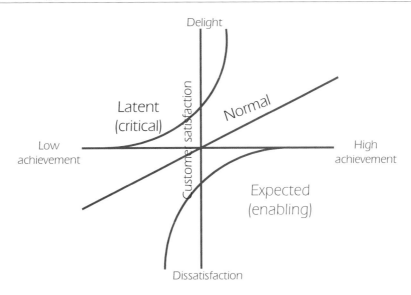

The difference between the two factors could also be expressed as the difference between an 'expected' factor and a 'latent' factor. Both are usually unspoken and unexpressed but in separate ways – important.

Where the two axes cross and for some distance around them the customer requirement is 'normal'. Customers usually state their needs in this area and by meeting them it is possible to move them closer to delight.

Enabling

Where an enabling (expected) factor is present customers do not even realize consciously – eg they 'expect it to be there' and it goes 'unnoticed'. If it is missing, however, customers complain about its absence. Good examples of this include: low platforms on buses – which are easy to get on and off; automatic doors in shopping centres; and outside-line availability tone on telephones – which elicit complaints where it takes more than one (nano) second. Unfortunately by concentrating on these factors the result – according to Dr Kano's analysis – is merely to reduce (or more likely to obviate) dissatisfaction. Failure to meet these requirements will result in unspoken rejection – ie they will be dissatisfied. While reducing these levels of dissatisfaction is clearly something that you must do – it will not increase loyalty nor increase delight.

Critical

By contrast focusing on critical factors enables you to move the customer into a delighted status and also to increase loyalty. Often these critical factors are unknown and therefore unspoken. As a result customers are not dissatisfied because they are not expecting them to be fulfilled. For example if asked (before the Sony Walkman was invented) virtually no customers would have articulated a need for 'music on the move' but after it was brought to market sales took off geometrically.

One issue with such factors of course is that eventually they become hygiene factors and are assumed to be in place. Eg air conditioning in cars sold in Europe is fast becoming standard (in the USA and other countries it has long been a standard feature) and CD players are going the same way. Another good example of this was the 'post-it' note. Nobody could have expressed exactly what it was that they wanted – but after it was 'discovered' by 3M it became globally ubiquitous. The 'post-it' note met a latent need and was a great success – but now it is found in every office, school and home and is standard stationery.

Figure 21: Satisfying your customers (Kano diagram)

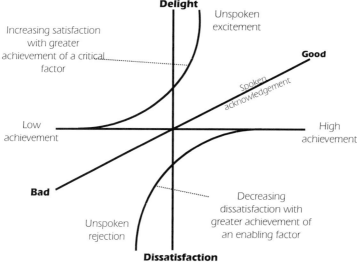

If we now plot the results of the possible actions it is possible to see that focusing on an enabling factor merely decreases the dissatisfaction whereas emphasis on critical factors really does add value and, therefore, increase loyalty. Focusing on normal factors gives spoken acknowledgement but does not necessarily lead to increasing delight.

The message from this analysis is that you must understand the difference between these factors and tailor your offering accordingly. While there may be some general trends – they will differ between customers and the use of Customer Relationship Management is critical in assisting in this understanding.

4.6 Measuring customer views on features

Obtaining customers views on features in often carried out but also frequently insufficiently analysed. This is because the research tries to use very complicated methods such as conjoint analysis. This is where respondees are asked to state which feature they prefer over another. There are several questions in the same mode and the results are then analysed and correlated – using serious computing power. For example with respect to a car they may be asked – 'do you prefer air conditioning to a CD player?'. They may then be asked if they prefer 'a CD player to a sun roof?' or whether they prefer 'electronic windows to air conditioning?' and so on. The objective is to ascertain the key preferences in priority.

It is possible, however, to ask your customers how they feel about features or services and undertake simple analysis by tabulating them to enable you to understand what moves them into delight or not. The method adopted is usually to ask the same question in both the positive form and the negative form[4]. The respondee is offered a choice of four responses.

For example:

- What do you feel if our service includes 'X'? [positive]
- What do you feel if our service does not include 'X'? [negative]

Responses:

1. I like it

2. It is a normal feature (ie expected)

3. I am indifferent

4. I don't like it

The answers are then tabulated and those features that have high cross-correlation will be those that you should concentrate on:

---

[4]   Dr Eva Chen: Paper1992 'Understanding Customer Requirements: Development of Metrics'

Figure 22: Measuring Satisfaction

		Answers to Negative Question			
		Like	Normal	Indifferent	Don't Like
Answers to Positive Question	Like		Delight	Delight	Normal
	Normal				Expected
	Indifferent				Expected
	Don't Like				

Case study: Konica

In the 70s Konica realized that to remain competitive it required a new camera that was perceived as radically differentiated from what was available at the time, yet Konica's sales and research groups reported that customers were asking for only minor modifications to the existing model. They turned to Dr Kano for advice.

Kano stated that success was to not just listen to what customers were *saying* but to develop a deep understanding of the customer's environment and then address those unspoken and unexpressed but nevertheless real needs. In order to achieve this Konica sent employees to commercial photo processing labs to examine customers' photographs.

What they found were many problems such as under/over exposure, blurred images, etc due to the majority of customers being unable to take pictures properly as the cameras (which contained features that customers had asked for and functionality that was considered normal) were too complicated to use effectively. Konica set itself the goal of addressing these issues in order to improve its camera and meet customers' unspoken needs (to take reasonable quality pictures with minimum effort). The resolution of these issues resulted in new features – which of course are now commonly considered as standard (hygiene factors) for a camera – autofocus, built-in-flash, automatic film winding.

Key learning points

1. Customer Relationship Management must support whatever strategy the organization has.

2. Research has shown that the most common reason for changing suppliers driven by internal factors is poor service, therefore, service quality is critical to customer retention via Customer Relationship Management.

3. Customers' expectations of service and quality have changed and they are not only less tolerant generally of errors but also much more likely to leave as a result as there is now much greater choice and a greater understanding of the market.

4. It is necessary to understand which items are regarded as 'critical' factors by customers and which are merely 'enabling' factors. Focusing on your customers' critical factors enables you to move the customer into a delighted status and also to increase loyalty.

Further reading

Shiv Mathur & Alfred Kenyon: *Creating Value* (part III)

Peter Doyle: *Value-based Marketing*

5

CUSTOMER RELATIONSHIP MANAGEMENT – HISTORICAL DEVELOPMENT

Topics in this chapter

- Beginnings
- Four Ps v. four Cs
- Ansoff matrix
- Delighting customers

Syllabus topics covered

- Consumer behaviour principles.
- Organizational buying behaviour.
- Retail and business customer profiling.
- Relationship life cycles.
- Understanding and managing customer expectations.
- Building relationships by adding value to customers cost effectively.

Introduction

Customer Relationship Management is founded in marketing and is focused very much on the customer perspective. Marketing has not always taken this focus and has only relatively recently moved from 'selling' mode to true 'marketing' based on a real understanding of customer needs.

5.1   Historical antecedents

Marketing has its roots in production and then sales. Everything started with the perception that there was a need and that the 'entrepreneur' could produce something to fulfill that need. In the early days of 'mercantilism' this was not incorrect; however, with the increasing sophistication of buyers and the growth of similar products and substitutes, this basic premise changed.

Traditionally, therefore, organizations were internally focused – ie they would say 'what do we make/offer, and how do we sell it?' This lead to the rise of product-focused marketing and the four Ps[5]:

Product	**Price**
Promotion	**Place**

For many years these four elements were the cornerstone of marketing for everyone and collectively are known as:

The marketing mix

It is the different blends of these four elements that enable organizations to differentiate their products from competitors' (in theory at least). These four aspects of what you offer must be aligned with your Customer Value Propositions – and will be different for each offering and each segment. Different offerings take different mixes of these four.

A major retailer will always want to be in the best location – eg a high street or major shopping centre because they rely on high footfall to sell lots of goods. Other retailers will have different views on this and will be prepared to take less prominent locations because they feel it will not materially affect their business – perhaps they sell by word of mouth or through other mechanisms (mail). With increasing mobility of the population in the UK and increased usage of cars to shop once a week instead of daily many retailers are now responding to these demographic changes and moving to out-of-town locations. There is more space and they can not only offer a more extensive range of goods but also offer parking and additionally sell petrol, thus increasing turnover and profit considerably (extra sales, lower costs – greater economies of scale) **(Place)**

Similarly while some organizations sell by offering the cheapest ('pile it high and sell it cheap') others play on different subtleties and are very expensive. There are, however, perceived pricing 'bands' outside of which goods will not sell. If you go to any shop the price of a basic commodity such as butter, although it will vary both within the shop by brand, and between that shop and others, will be within a pretty small range. This is because nobody pays £100 for a packet of butter, because at that price it falls well outside of the 'band' with which almost everyone is familiar. For other goods such as wine, however, it is a completely different picture. You can buy a bottle of 'rot-gut' for less than £1 but you can also pay hundreds of pounds for a fine wine such as a Chateau D'Yquem. Many people are also unsure of the price bands for such goods and therefore often pay much more than they ought to. **(Price)**

These are explored in more detail overleaf.

---

[5] E Jerome McCarthy: *Basic Marketing: A Managerial Approach* (Homewood IL:Irwin 1960)

Product

This is the substance of what you are offering. It may be one thing or several things bundled together as a solution – eg for a corporate customer – Loan, Overdraft, F/X, Guarantees and Trade Finance limits all together as sub-components of an overall limit. In the case of a personal customer an overdraft may be linked to a personal loan and a mortgage; often with life insurance thrown in. It also includes services if that is your market – eg consultancy, legal advice, painting and decorating. The key factors here are:

- **Customer benefits** – special items;

- **Quality** – how good is it really – Rolls-Royce versus Reliant Robin;

- **Design** – basic vanilla – comprehensive/complex derivatives;

- **Technical features** – bells and whistles;

- **Branding** (in-house, white label, 'cachet' – multi-brands within one organization – Lloyds/TSB/Cheltenham & Gloucester/Abbey Life);

- **Packaging** – how it looks or is presented;

- **Service** that accompanies it (follow-up, customer helpline etc);

- **Training** – eg in software given to clients for cashflow purposes.

Price

What you charge for your goods. There are many ways of pricing including

Market-based and cost-based, but these are driven by internal considerations. You can also set price by reference to competitors' pricing (eg base rates are very rarely out of line for good reasons because money soon flows into those organizations offering the highest deposit rates and out of those with lower rates who in turn are besieged by demands for cheap loans which soon moves the balance sheet returns into disequilibrium) or by what you think the market will bear – often useful if you enjoy a monopoly. It is related to product and offering less value for more price is not usually a winning combination. Price… 'has a major influence on the volume of sales that you are likely to achieve, and thus influences both sales revenue and profit'[6].

Price is very flexible and you can vary it more than the others because it is usually within your discretion (for some services this may not be the case – eg mortgage rate is often set centrally with no discretion in branches – however local staff can sometimes flex fees) and you can use it for long-term and also short-term advantage. Some possibilities include:

- **discounts** for special customers (ex-ante price reductions);

- **underselling** or matching competitors (eg John Lewis Partnership – 'Never Knowingly Undersold');

- **loyalty refunds** (eg Britannia Building Society 'Members Loyalty Bonus Scheme' or the Co-op 'Divi') (ex-post price reductions);

[6] Richard Collier: *Profitable Product Management* (CIM/Butterworth Heinemann 1995)

- **bundling** items together and offering overall prices – eg three services which each might cost 3.0% pa, together may cost only 7.5% as a bundle.

Although price is not (necessarily) a measure of inherent value received, it is often used by customers as a benchmark, ignoring any other features or differences. (This can be irritating but it is the customer's perception that counts and the job of the relationship manager to clarify the misunderstanding and to change this perception by making them understand the differentials.)

It should also be remembered that Price is the only one that brings in income.

All the rest involve cost!

Promotion

How you get the message across to your potential customers. It is all very well having something to sell to customers but you have got to get it across to them in a manner that is cost-effective. Some of the more usual methods include:

- **Advertising** – on the radio, TV, in papers or magazines and increasingly on the Internet – indirectly on someone else's or on your own website, or via linking to a search engine;

- **Telephone selling** – effective but can quickly become an irritant if poorly executed – eg employment agencies calling up once or twice every day;

- **Brochures** and catalogues;

- **Exhibitions** and third-party endorsement;

- **Sales force** (eg man from the Pru);

- **Billboards** and other similar methods – fly posters;

- **Window posters** are very effective and a common feature in, for example, building societies

- **Leaflets** – can be indiscriminate – (eg given out in the street or put on cars) or more targeted – despatched with statement – and/or linked to an event – (eg 'your policy reaches its tenth anniversary or matures – why not deposit the funds in our new account that pays you x%?' etc). They can also be extremely cost-effective – they are cheap to produce and when targeted – eg a take-away curry house that leaflets dwellings within its delivery area – can yield substantial returns;

- **Face-to-face** – eg by cashiers when a customer enters the branch – 'have you had an account review recently?' – 'I notice that you are travelling to the Gulf – have you taken out life and travel insurance?'

- **'best-buy' tables** – where one of your products or services appears at the top of a value for money table which generates publicity.

It is vital that the message stands out from the clutter of everyday rubbish that assaults us continually.

NB

> *PR is different, and is about name or organizational branding awareness, ie getting the name of an organization (eg Barclays, HSBC, Stroud & Swindon, Derbyshire, Prudential or CGNU) in the press or other media (in favourable circumstances).*

Place

This is about getting your product in front of your customers. It used to be called 'location, location, location' – however newer channels, which are generally remote, render this analysis largely redundant. It is really about distribution channels and these are extremely complex now. You may sell directly remotely, directly face-to-face, via third-party branches (agencies) through a sales force, via the Internet, through the telephone via 'warehouses' or third-party agencies – eg lead managers in syndications, co-joint lending etc, or you may be servicing other organization's portfolios and trying to sell them your services as well.

Different channels may require different (or seemingly different) products and services but beware differential pricing rules and regulations.

4P summary

This was where the theory and subsequent practice was focused – on looking at how you sold what you had to the market. For many organizations this still holds true. Unfortunately it is based on a premise that is increasingly coming to be regarded as false – that which states that if I produce something I just need to market it correctly and people will buy it.

5.2   New horizons in marketing

As further analysis has taken place, however, and greater understanding of buyers' behaviour has been realized, there has been a fundamental shift from the traditional product-focused, internal view to an externally-focused, customer-centric view. Marketing theory has, accordingly, changed to looking at, analysing and understanding things from the buyer's – ie customers' – perspective.

This is a totally different viewpoint from the historical perspective and (while still anathema to many marketing people) is now generally recognized as the better viewpoint.

This has lead to the emergence of a new understanding of buying behaviours – called the four Cs[7] –which looks at the buying cycle from the **Customers'** viewpoint and gives a different perspective which can be summarized as:

Cost	**Convenience**
Customer needs and wants	**Communication.**

[7]   Robert Lauterborn: 'New Marketing Litany' (article in *Advertising Age* October 1990)

Figure 23: 4 Ps versus 4 Cs

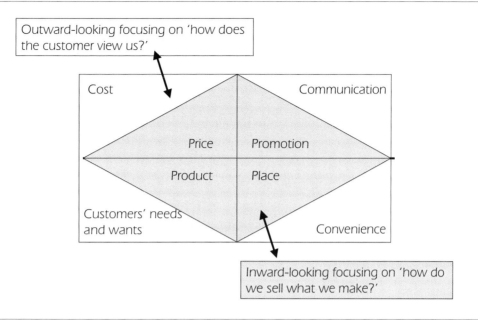

This view seeks to be **outside looking in** rather than **inside looking out**. What is it that the customer thinks about the offering and what makes him buy it – or why does he not?

Cost

This represents the cost to him if he takes your product or service. He does not pay a *price* in his perception but incurs a *cost* (see Customer Value Proposition), ie not only what he has to pay but what he has to forego in order to obtain your product. This could include intangible and non-physical issues such as time spent, foreign exchange needed, comparisons of quality or value and other things done before even any money changes hands. Customers will put a cost on non-cash effort even if they cannot quantify it absolutely.

Convenience

This is more than just what is called 'location' (ie where you as a supplier are or where your outlets are situated) but from the customers' viewpoint – what is the easiest way to get hold of the good or service required, or to deal with a query, or resolve an problem. Customers are often prepared to trade off a lot for convenience. This might, for instance, include using different channels rather than bricks and mortar branch networks. You might spend a lot in informing your customer base that your service is the best but if the only cashpoint in the village belongs to a competitor then they will use that one and not go to the nearest outlet of your organization because it is more convenient – even where there is an extra cost involved (provided it is not too great).

What seems intuitive to you will not to them (we see bank customers queuing outside in the rain at ATMs when cashiers have nothing to do inside) – and with the sweeping changes to electronic sales and advertising; what is the 10-year NPV of a branch network? – in many cases it is negative! Similarly the changes demand different skills – no longer is customer-handling a prerequisite, it is now fast, timely, error-free delivery

Customer needs and wants

These two things are different and it is important to understand the difference. **Needs** are real – **wants** are aspirational. For example I would *like* **(want)** a mansion in the country but I *require* somewhere to live that is within my budget **(need)**.

This will mean that *no matter what the customer may look at*, she will buy what she needs, at a price that she can afford.

It is possible, however, to sell something to someone by seemingly focusing on their wants, and often marketing is couched in this way. The closer that you can align your offering that meets the customers' **needs** to the customers' **wants**, then the more likely you are to succeed in persuading the customer to buy your particular offering. The more that you can supply something that meets (or partly meets) a **want,** but at a price that is closer to the **need**, then the greater your probability of success will be. This difference between **wants** and **needs** is known as a **'perception gap'** and is important in understanding your customers.

Figure 24: Price-Value trade-off

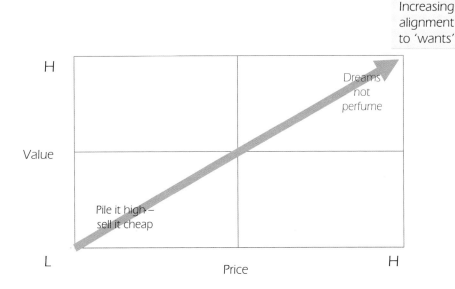

When selling anything there is a price/value trade-off. Customers will pay highly for something that they believe adds value to their lives – even if it is not necessarily so (dreams not perfume) whereas if they think it is a commodity then they will differentiate only on price.

For example customers may come in and say '…I want service X'… but this may be inappropriate for them (too expensive, does not deliver what they want – you might not have it). By understanding the underlying need, however, you can develop an offering that will satisfy them and by customizing it to meet as much of their aspirations as possible you may lock them in for longer than with a basic commodity purchase.

Case Study: 'What colour is your card?'

American Express started off with the ordinary 'green card' and marketed it strongly, with many campaigns aimed at promoting it as the thing to have (**'don't leave home without it'**). Amex was pursuing the theory of increasing 'Market share'. Unfortunately this rapid and massive (and successful) expansion had its adverse reactions. As its success grew some people felt it was no longer a privilege to have one – as anyone could – and they started looking to other cards (eg Visa and Mastercard etc.) and its share of premium customers fell – even though Amex had increased its base enormously. They then introduced a 'Gold card' for premium customers to reflect their need to be different. This enabled then to re-capture premium customers.

More recently they have introduced the 'Blue card' aimed at younger people who want to be associated with **'cool and trendy'** living and be visibly seen to be different from the other green or even gold holders. For those at the top end of the market they also have the 'Black card' – for those who have great wealth and high spending habits. Each card comes with different range of services and privileges. They also have corporate cards aimed at companies' staff. This is highly-focused targeting of customers and meeting their needs and wants by differentiating the services offered. Other companies have followed suit with their own gold, platinum or silver cards.

One of the objectives of a Customer Relationship Management programme must be to provide information to staff to understand this perception, how it affects their customers and to enable them to capitalize on it when offering services.

Communication

This is about getting your message to the customer – and getting it to stand out from the clutter and background noise which surrounds it. A golden rule here is to focus your communication on your customers' (segmented) wants and needs. Instead of viewing it as promoting your product – think of it as an exercise in communicating a value proposition to your customers and prospective customers. Why should they listen/read it? Focus on their needs and wants and customize the contents to them. You would not usually advertise in the

Greek language in France (unless you were targeting ex-patriate Greeks) – because no-one would understand it and it would be wasted. Apply that analogy to any communication and you will soon see why the customer focus is key.

Marketing

Customer Relationship Management then is about shifting the emphasis from *selling* to *marketing* and using different strategies, tactics and approaches to increase your share of the customers' spend.

In the classic Ansoff matrix[8], shown below, this would be classed as quartile 1 – **market penetration** – ie selling more into your existing market (customers) by understanding their needs, linked with judicious forays into quartiles 2 and 3 – extending your product penetration and developing new customers.

Figure 25: Marketing/risk assessment matrix (Ansoff)

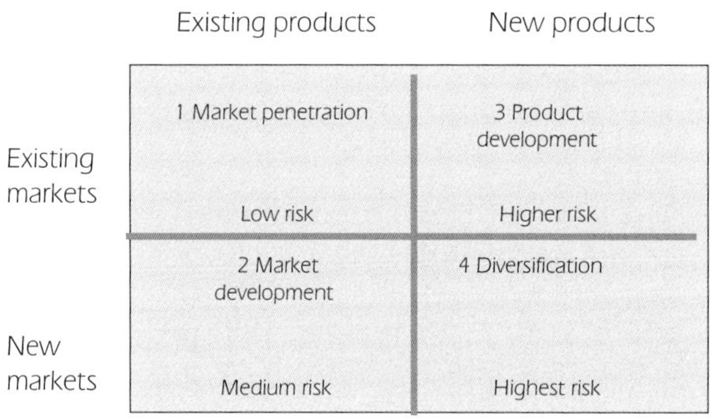

	Existing products	New products
Existing markets	1 Market penetration Low risk	3 Product development Higher risk
New markets	2 Market development Medium risk	4 Diversification Highest risk

Need to formulate your own strategy and understand your competitors'
likely response and what the risk is therefrom

There are four types of marketing strategies, as shown in the diagram above.

Market penetration: where the objectives are to increase market share; increase sales to existing customers; make sales to new customers by selective price reductions; selling alternative services; accepting smaller orders; improve selling methods; improve customer service or add extra value (Customer Value Proposition equation must be equalized).

Market development: where you must segment current market; focus different blends of services at different segments; price by segment; develop new markets.

Product/service development: change current services; develop new services; new capabilities and enhance current services; change service mix; unbundle services and premium price.

[8] Igor Ansoff: *Strategic Planning* (Penguin)

Diversification: acquire a supplier; acquire a distributor; enter a new area of expertise; brand extension; service extension or exit some markets and re-focus.

Key learning points

1. Customer Relationship Management is founded in marketing and is focused very much on the customer perspective.

2. There is a new understanding of buying behaviours – called the four Cs which looks at the buying cycle from the **Customers'** viewpoint and gives a different perspective which can be summarized as: **Cost, Convenience, Customer needs and wants, and Communication**.

3. **Needs** are real – **wants** are aspirational. This will mean that *no matter what the customer may talk about*, she will buy what she needs, at a price that she can afford.

4. The **Price-Value** trade-off that a customer makes is not just about money and involves other less tangible issues. You must understand this to make effective offerings.

5. Market penetration – ie selling more to your existing customer base is a much less risky strategy than market or product diversification and is generally a better return on investment.

Further reading

Ansoff: *Strategic Planning*

Kotler: *Principles of Marketing*

Russell-Jones, Fletcher: *Marketing Pocketbook*

6

CUSTOMER RELATIONSHIP MANAGEMENT IN FINANCIAL SERVICES

Topics in this chapter

- Why it is different
- Customer diversity
- Lessons from elsewhere

Syllabus topics covered

- The importance of effective Customer Relationship Management strategies as an integral part of effective financial services.
- The business environment of Customer Relationship Management: legal, ethical, economic, competitive and social.

Introduction

Financial services is different from many other industries for a number of reasons:

- It covers the whole spectrum of customers from individuals through partnerships, unincorporated bodies, institutions, corporates and governments as well as other financial institutions. As a result it can be very difficult to focus on single markets – especially as they are often intertwined

- Understanding the value chain is complex because customers are often suppliers at the same time (eg they may have deposit and savings accounts as well as loans and overdrafts)

- It deals only in intangibles – not products – so it is, therefore, very service focused

- The customer relationship is usually multi-product and multi-channel (and almost invariably multi-system)

- It requires to process billions and billions of transactions worldwide

- It is one of the most heavily regulated industries in the world

The financial services sector is largely people- and relationship-based, although there has been a move to commoditize some products and services (mortgages, personal loans etc). Where products have become commodities they tend to be bought on the basis of price and it is very difficult to differentiate. You must, therefore, differentiate through other means such as the quality of 'after sales' or 'delivery' service.

In addition customers in the financial services sector are generally:

- more techno-literate
- better informed
- used to greater choice
- switching channels
- more demanding of service
- used to change

…and markets are changing at a progressively increasing pace:

- channel substitution is well advanced
- cheap technology enables new entrants
- new technology disintermediates brands (eg Internet icons) – you are only a 'click' away from your competition
- political agendas also influence trends (the advent of the European single currency 'euro' will change the face of European and possibly other banking markets fundamentally)

Because financial services organizations, by and large, deal with all aspects of the chain, including personal customers; self-employed business people; partnerships; corporates – large and small; Government entities; mutual organizations and indeed other banks, the customer base is extremely diverse and accordingly they all have different needs, requirements and demands.

Even within each category there are different needs. Consider corporates – a manufacturer may require support for:

- Raw materials finance
- Work in progress finance
- Debtor funding

(In fact classic working capital funding)

If they export or import then they may require

- Trade finance

- Foreign exchange

- Guarantees

- Overseas banking facilities

- etc

A local authority, however, will have very different needs and be driven by different issues:

- they have lumpy cashflows

  - because some residents pay monthly, quarterly, semi-annually

  - indeed some do not pay at all or very late

  - some pay in cash, perhaps weekly

  - some pay via standing order/direct debits etc

- rate payers also vote and local authorities are usually (sometimes) concerned about factors that affect them

- they are concerned about costs of internal processing

- they worry about external (bank) charges

- they have regular payments to make

It is, therefore, necessary to understand your customers' needs extremely well and work with them to develop relationships and tailor the services precisely to their differing needs *and* their customers' needs.

Case study: Design and development of cahoot's CRM system

Background

In 1998 Forrester, a leading research company for Electronic Commerce, predicted that within five years, no traditional bank would survive without an effective answer to Electronic Commerce, because financial services, telecommunications and retailing were at the epicentre of a deep economic change.

The UK financial services market had gained a reputation for being 'over-banked', with too many participants, however, UK banking still remained very profitable even for smaller banks. On-line banking seemed to fall into two camps – those that were merely additional channels for a mainstream bank (such as Barclays and Lloyds TSB) and those that had a separate on-line identity (such as Egg and First-e).

The Abbey National response to the above challenge included the launch of Project Aquarius in September 1998; a small management team which was formed from visionary Abbey National staff which set out with the intention of leading the future of banking.

The new standalone bank would be targeted at the mass-affluent actor - aged 25-54, with household incomes above £25,000, those who were technology-confident, but time-poor. The proposition would be based on customer centricity and ease of use, while placing the customer more fully in control of his finances than previously possible. Aquarius would be seen as an innovative and comprehensive solution to modern banking needs.

Project Aquarius was re-named cahoot, and opened for business on 12 June 2000. Since then, cahoot has gone on to win awards, including the Gomez Online Credit Card in Autumn and Winter 2000 and IVCA Best Business to Consumer Transactional Website.

Channels

The primary access channel to cahoot is the Internet, which will soon be complemented by digital television. Customers may also perform (limited) banking through their WAP phones and using Interactive Voice Response (IVR). A 24-hour contact centre supports IVR, calls to live agents, e-mail messaging and some fulfilment. In addition, cahoot offers services via Automatic Teller Machines and the Post Office. The bank makes outbound communications through a variety of channels, including e-mail, SMS messaging, the telephone and secure message boards (which customers may view on the cahoot banking site).

Products and pricing

When the bank first launched it, it offered two products – a current account and a credit card. An unsecured loan and structured savings products were later added to the portfolio. cahoot is committed to individual pricing; according to risk for new customers and to risk and value for its existing customers. As a low-cost bank with customers visiting via the Internet and managing their accounts and transactions through automated processes, cahoot is able to offer market leading rates to its customers. cahoot also offers products such as insurances provided by partner companies and links to other partner companies.

Architecture

The great challenge for Information Technology was to develop a robust solution in a timely manner, thus allowing cahoot to take early-mover advantage. The architecture is component-based with individual components resting on flexible rules-based systems. The architecture was designed to allow the easy addition of new products and channels and for straightforward scalability.

cahoot's service is based on IBM's Corepoint Banking System solution and integrated with back-end transaction processing systems – VisionPlus from Paysys and ICBS from Fiserv and utilising Blaze Advisor, the front-end decisioning tool. Alliant, from Fiserv provides the contact centre's channel integration and customer servicing solution. Analytical, reporting and campaign management tools work on the data warehouse, Fiserv's InformEnt.

cahoot CRM strategy

The basic principle underpinning the cahoot CRM strategy is that customers will be managed in such a way as to maintain or increase their value to the bank. Customer relationships will be analysed and monitored from many perspectives and strategies employed to manage individual customer values by leveraging behaviour, offering individual pricing and products, influencing channel usage etc.

cahoot CRM system

Having made the decision for sound business reasons to build a component-based bank, the challenges ahead for CRM lay in bringing together data from the many source components, holding it at the customer level and offering one view of the customer at all touch-points.

Data warehouse

The data warehouse sits at the heart of the cahoot CRM strategy, and is updated every day from the source systems. Since the build first commenced, more and more data has been mapped into the warehouse, thus giving an ever more detailed picture of each customer relationship. The various data sources are described below:

- Application database – potential customers complete the on-line application form, and after a check with a credit reference agency, the decision engine will either conditionally accept or reject that application. The information held in the application database includes personal details, product selections, details about other financial relationships, given credit scores and advertising media source.

- Product systems – the various product systems hold product details and transactional information at the product level. While most variables had been mapped at the time of launch, a great deal of subsequent work has been done in capturing these variables at specified periods of time, rolling them up to customer level and mapping into trending tables within the warehouse, thus allowing an accessible, historical picture of each customer's banking behaviour.

- Web logs – both the public (marketing) and private (banking) sites have their own web logs, joined by a cross-reference file. Each click that customers make on-line is captured by the web logs, thus allowing cahoot to track their exact journeys. The challenge has been to cut through the mass of data and decide what elements will be of importance, and then to store them at the customer level in easily accessible tables.

- Contact history – every time a customer contacts the contact centre, perhaps by telephone, using IVR or by e-mail, certain elements of that communication will be captured within contact logs and subsequently stored within the warehouse. Likewise, details will be held about outbound communications sent either by the contact centre or the Customer Management system. It has been important to ensure that contact centre agents adhere strictly to the contact log completion processes so that the data allows an accurate analysis of contacts.

- Channel usage – customers may transact from their accounts through a variety of channels – perhaps the web (including Digital TV in the near future), WAP phone or an ATM. Likewise, they may select a channel in order to change their personal details or make certain requests. It is important to understand which channels given customers are using for which actions.

● External data – cahoot receives regular feeds of data about each customer from a Credit Risk Agency. In addition, it has access to most of the popular geo-demographic systems.

Statistical analysis and modelling

The complement of analytical and modelling tools has been enhanced since the bank first launched. During the early days the emphasis was on straightforward business information such as number of accounts and customers and the size of asset and liability. As time has passed and historical data has been generated, statistical analysis and modelling tools have come into their own. All such tools sit upon the data warehouse and have been set up in such a way that they can easily access the full spectrum of customer data. Key staff may perform any modelling and analyses from their desktops or from anywhere else that they may choose to access the network.

● Business reporting – most of cahoot's business reporting is generated by tools, such as KnowledgeShare (also known as Brio), working on the data warehouse. Routine reports have been set up on a schedule for delivery to the business owners. In addition, most business users have easy access to the warehouse through KnowledgeShare and may build their own *ad hoc* reports as required.

● Analysis and modelling – one of the key uses of the analytical tools will be to segment the customer base. The initial development of the customer behavioural segmentation will include some basic application and transactional data only. Once this is complete further data will be added, bit by bit, to enrich the customer picture. At the same time analysts are concentrating on trying to understand the value associated with customer behaviour and will produce a value overlay to work with the customer segmentation.

The implementation of segmental strategies will provide the framework for the management of customers and business decisions made across the bank – including new product development, channel development and decisions about the allocation of resource.

Campaign management

MarketShare (also known as Protagona) was selected as the campaign management tool for cahoot, and is used to generate most of the bank's automated communications. The campaign management staff have desktop access to MarketShare and are able to build customer campaigns with little, often no, support from their IT colleagues.

MarketShare is flexible enough to manage both operational and marketing communications (campaigns) for the bank. Once the campaigns have been built, they may be deployed manually or placed on a schedule to run automatically. The campaign management tool searches the data for instances where the campaign triggers have been met, and automatically sends the relevant message through the selected channel to the given customer. A variety of channels are available for message distribution, including personalized e-mail, SMS and customers' secure message boards. In addition, mailing or telephone call lists may be generated.

Trigger alerts

One of cahoot's most popular features is the trigger alerts. Customers may select to receive one of these five alerts through e-mail and/or SMS. The message will also be sent to their secure message board. These alerts have been built as campaigns in MarketShare and run on a daily schedule. With message options such as 'please tell me when the balance on any of my current accounts is below this amount', customers are able to manage their finances with the minimum of hassle and worry.

Customer decisions

The bank will continually make decisions about its customers – perhaps who to offer a credit limit increase to and by how much, or which customers have above a given propensity to take a certain product and at what rate that should be offered. Decisions such as these are made at the back-end, by one or more of the modelling, analytical or campaign management tools. The front-end decision engine will use its rules to make decisions about applicants and customers whilst they are using the web or other customer touch-points. One of the big challenges that cahoot faced was to ensure a seamless integration of the front- and back-end decisions so that back-end decisions were available, in particular to the web and contact centre.

Customer segmentation

The implementation of customer segmentation will allow the business as a whole to treat different customers differently according to the segment strategy. The segment code (current and historical) will be stored in the warehouse at the customer level and thus be available to the analysis, modelling and campaign management tools. In this way customer segment will influence all decisions about customers made at the back-end. There is also a requirement to have the segment code available, in particular, to front-end decisioning at the web and to the contact centre.

The future

Having gathered a critical mass of current and historical data, cahoot has started on the journey of interpreting the results of analyses and modelling work. The build of the required functionality to have the output available to all customer touch-points and to allow the bank to treat different customers differently is well underway. The business managers are united in the desire to ensure customer centricity and the development of a valuable customer base and so will champion the use of the above data and functionality as it becomes available.

Source: cahoot (Abbey National)

The market is also highly competitive and new entrants are coming in every day from diverse sources. Players in the market, depending on your own particular niche, might include:

Domestic Banks

Foreign banks in the UK

Overseas banks

Building societies and other mutuals

Credit card/charge card companies

Insurance companies

Corporates

Utilities

Retailers

Department stores

Energy companies

Telecomms companies

etc

Figure 26

UNI STOREBRAND PLANS NEW
COMMERCIAL BANK (Norway)

THE PRU TAKES ON BANKS
AND BUILDING SOCIETIES (UK)

SONAE TO LAUNCH ITS OWN BANK -
UNIVERSO BANCO DIRECTO (Portugal)

BANKS ARE LIKE DINOSAURS (Microsoft - USA)

OUR CORE BUSINESS IS BEING THREATENED
BY RIVALS WE NEVER KNEW BEFORE (Deutsche Bank - Germany)

VIRGIN DIRECT TO
SELL PENSIONS (UK)

TESCO HAS WATCHED THE BANKS
AND THINKS MOST ARE A BUNCH
OF CLOWNS ... (Tesco - UK)

MBNA AND FIRST USA, BOTH NON-BANK CREDIT CARD
SPECIALISTS, LEAD THE US CREDIT CARD BUSINESS (USA)

It is necessary to understand your competition – but not at the macro level; this should be completed as part of the strategic process. What is needed in the context of Customer Relationship Management is an understanding of the competition for your own particular customers – and their offerings and their respective strengths. If you are offering products to personal customers or small business:

- who else is in the market locally?

- how strong are they and what are their products like?

- how do they compete – price, quality, service?

- do they belong to a larger group or are they wholly local (eg regional banks or building societies)?

This is where capture of data within the Customer Relationship Management system is so important. The Sun Tzu matrix[9] below shows the increasing likelihood of success where you know your own strengths and those of your enemy (competition).

Figure 27: Sun Tzu matrix

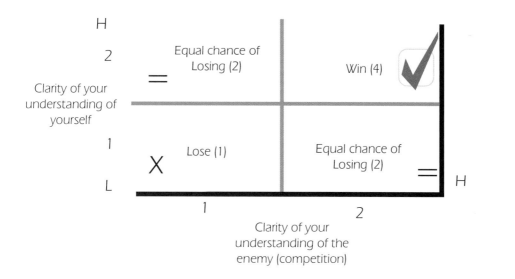

Market understanding

It is also necessary to consider the marketplace as well and in particular what the key factors are affecting profitability and stability. The special needs of each marketplace affect the ability to enter. Barriers come in all sorts of sizes and shapes. They can include legislation, capital requirements, skills location etc. The existence of patents is a very effective barrier to entry because no-one else can produce your product, although where patents are not universal you may get 'parallel imports' (see Tesco's legal fight to import 'designer jeans').

The threat of retaliation can also be a very effective deterrent. Some years ago one of the leading US manufacturers of disposable razors decided to attack Bic in its home market (Continental Europe). The retaliation was bitter and based on price and successfully drove the American attacker out very quickly.

---

[9] Sun Tzu: *The Art of War* (Hodder & Stoughton)

Some markets are easy to enter – recruitment, for example, where you just need an office and a few telephones plus a few contacts. To enter the oil industry however is a different thing altogether and is extremely difficult. This is because of the specific barriers – you need to acquire oil wells or at least the outputs, you may need to build petroleum cracking plants etc.

Financial services has been made much easier to enter in recent years due to the easing of legislation covering many aspects of its business – although still subject to heavy regulation in an operational sense. Some industries also have high barriers to exit – either from capital disinvestments – who wants to buy a second-hand petroleum cracking plant? Or how do you run off a 20-year insurance portfolio?

Case study: First Direct

First Direct was a new venture by Midland Bank – now part of HSBC – but then a separate UK clearing bank. It saw an opportunity in the market for direct (at that stage telephone) banking in the 80s and established a new subsidiary. It also recognized the need for it to be separate and gave a great deal of carte blanche to the team. This paid dividends as it is now one of the most successful direct banks offering 24/7 service to customers. Polls of customers showed 87% of its base was extremely or very satisfied with it, a staggering proportion given that most banks struggle to achieve 50%. Similarly 85% of its customers would or had recommended it highly to others. Part of its success is that it is highly automated, based on call centre and Customer Relationship Management principles and was an early Greenfield site. The other part of its success was that applicants are thoroughly screened and those that it considers unprofitable for it (those which it calculated would generate low customer lifetime value) are rejected – ie it established prime mover advantage and was able to cherry pick its customers. Late followers of course would not have the same latitude.

The existence of barriers to entrance and exit affects the profit greatly. In combination they affect the levels of profitability and the stability of that profit. This is due to the ease – or difficulty – of new competition coming in (which tends to depress profit) and existing competition leaving (which would tend to increase profit).

Figure 28: The impact of barriers on profit

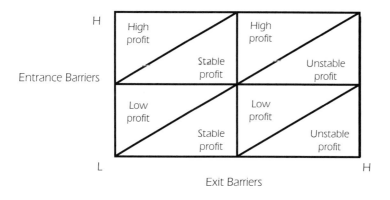

For example, where there are high barriers to entrance but low exit barriers this is the best of all worlds because the high entrance barriers mean that few new competitors come in to take market share and the low exit barriers mean that losers can get out easily and therefore enable remaining players to continue.

Where both entrance and exit barriers are high then while profit tends to be high it is also unstable because players who really should get out are forced to stay and this can mean that they may take pricing decisions which affect prices as they try to make the best of a bad hand.

With low entrance barriers **and** low exit barriers then – as new competitors can come and go easily – profits will always be low, but stable as people cut their losses and get out. To operate here it is critical to have either price advantage or some other reason for staying (cross subsidization etc).

The worse scenario is where it is easy to get in but difficult to get out – where the products are easy to sell but demand long-term commitment or local regulations or culture make it so. The recent very bad publicity for Marks & Spencer as it tried to divest from the Continent is a prime example of this.

Mortgages were in this field until the recent development of securitization and sales of mortgage books changed that paradigm. Here not only is profit low due to competition but also unstable and it is generally not an attractive market. Financial service players will be operating in a broad spectrum of these types of market and an understanding of this will help in both setting strategy and also in targeting customers through Customer Relationship Management programmes.

Legislation affecting financial services

Financial services is one of the most heavily regulated industries in the world. There is a constant stream of laws, rules and other issues emanating from, *inter alia*, domestic governments, supranational bodies such as the EU, and global bodies such as BIS. As a result there is a plethora of legislation that affects quotidian activities. On top of this each organization has its own 'business rules' (procedures) as well as the many self-regulation or 'voluntary' bodies that impact on the activities.

Key points include:

N2 – FSA moved into being the single regulator within the UK.

Consumer Credit Act – regulated agreements are covered by its contents.

Basle II – which will affect banking seriously in terms of risk and capital allocation.

Data Protection Act – which is of critical importance to anyone establishing a database.

Money Laundering – which affects the relationship with new customers.

Other subjects within the overall syllabus cover these aspects in great detail. Nevertheless you must be familiar with relevant legislation as it affects your organization. Any Customer Relationship Management issues will be influenced by the current regulations in force and offerings must reflect this.

Key learning points

1. Understanding the nature of the markets in which you operate is critical – because entrance and exit barriers affect profit dynamics.

2. The financial services sector is different from other sectors in that it is highly regulated and also largely people- and relationship-based.

3. Financial services organizations, by and large, deal with all aspects of the chain, and the customer base is extremely diverse and accordingly they all have different needs, requirements and demands.

Further reading

Michael Porter: *Competitive Strategy*

Dwight Ritter: *Relationship Banking* (Chapter 1)

7

IMPLICATIONS OF CUSTOMER RELATIONSHIP MANAGEMENT AND WHY SO MANY INITIATIVES FAIL

Topics in this chapter

- Integration of Customer Relationship Management with strategy, policy and tactics
- New paradigms in operating
- Remuneration
- Measuring effectiveness
- MIS
- Culture changes
- Planning
- Execution
- Organizational buy-in

Syllabus topics covered

- The role of Customer Relationship Management in business strategy.
- Understanding service quality.
- Planning and managing Customer Relationship Management projects.
- Measuring performance of Customer Relationship Management.

Introduction

Where an organization is about to embark on a Customer Relationship Management initiative – or indeed is thinking about so doing – it is of vital importance that it understand the implications of this for the organization. Effective Customer Relationship Management is not a quick fix.

Bad press and reporting on apparent project failures and overexposure of the Customer Relationship Management concept is starting to cause a backlash and many organizations are asking themselves 'Is Customer Relationship Management really capable of delivering the benefits?' There is a growing trend not to call Customer Relationship Management projects 'Customer Relationship Management' at all, because they lose credibility from the start. Where this has occurred it is typically because they were not thought through and commenced half-heartedly supported by poor analysis without having considered the structure, the needs and the real implications for an organization.

Figure 29: Key reasons for implementing a CRM programme

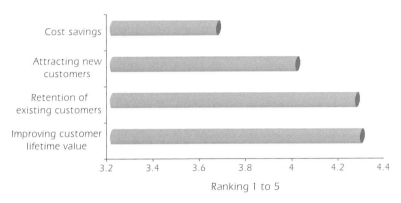

Source: PMP Research

A recent survey[10] analysed the thinking behind organizations starting a Customer Relationship Management programme. It showed that they were very clear as to the reasons – improving lifetime value and retention of customers. Of the organizations 14% were in financial services showing a clear understanding of the benefits.

For it to work properly, however, and to achieve the desired goals there is a lot that must be done before you even start implementing. The key issues for analysis include:

● What are our key objectives from a Customer Relationship Management initiative?

● How does that tie in with our stated strategy?

● What do we do currently in this context (do we really know)?

● What will we have to do (how can we tell)?

● What is the gap between these two states?

● What do we have to do to close the gap?

● Can we close the gap – is it feasible?

[10] Consultants Advisory Magazine – 'Customer Relationship Management' – June 2001.

● Can we do it ourselves – or should we buy in from external sources?

For most organizations they are unfortunately not starting with a clean sheet of paper. They will be looking at many systems which are a hodgepodge of various platforms supporting old, inefficient and fragmented processes with staff who are ill-equipped for the task ahead and who will also be inherently opposed to change by their very nature.

Figure 30: What does this mean?

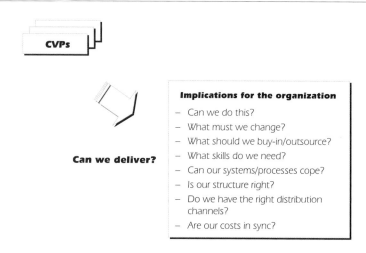

The gap will include the following items:

● Necessary system support

● Adequate information to populate the Customer Relationship Management

● The right staff

● With the right skills

● And the right training

Substantial benefits may be gained from Customer Relationship Management – they simply need more time, careful thought and planning. Also, the environmental forces of increased competition and consumer power mean that there is little choice for enterprises but to go on seeking the way to Customer Relationship Management. Customer Relationship Management goals can be achieved through dedicated planning and adherence to an enterprise vision and strategy. Based on this, architectures and technologies can be intelligently adopted and coordinated, and the appropriate skills and behaviours developed (see diagram over the page).

Figure 31: Details of analysis to understand CRM implications

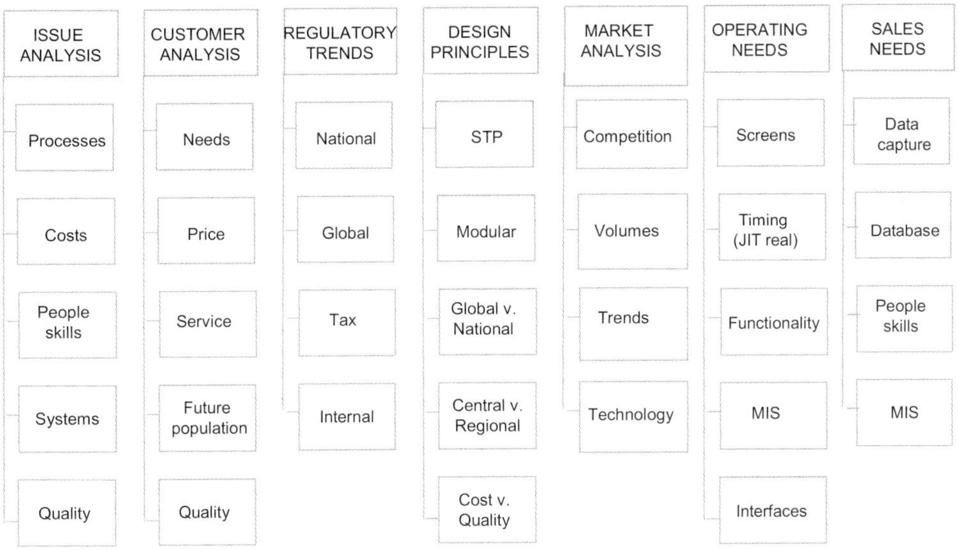

ISSUE ANALYSIS	CUSTOMER ANALYSIS	REGULATORY TRENDS	DESIGN PRINCIPLES	MARKET ANALYSIS	OPERATING NEEDS	SALES NEEDS
Processes	Needs	National	STP	Competition	Screens	Data capture
Costs	Price	Global	Modular	Volumes	Timing (JIT real)	Database
People skills	Service	Tax	Global v. National	Trends	Functionality	People skills
Systems	Future population	Internal	Central v. Regional	Technology	MIS	MIS
Quality	Quality		Cost v. Quality		Interfaces	

Customer Relationship Management has great implications for an organization – especially in terms of the following:

- People
- Processes
- Systems
- Structure

(and also strategy – because it both reflects strategic thinking and impacts upon it.)

People

Key questions here are:

- What type of people will we need?
- How many?
- What skills will they need – do we have them in house or do we need to import people – and when?
- What training will be needed – over what timescale – can we deliver it?
- What career development will be required?
- How do we manage it?

The financial services sector is very heavily people-based and sufficient attention must be placed on them. It is they that interface with customers and so they must be trained adequately with the right skills and attitudes.

There are many types of interface and you need to understand the nature and the magnitude of each member of staff's interactions with customers. There are four types:

'Interfacers'

'Interjacents'

'Interfusers' and

'Interplayers'.

The diagram below shows their respective involvement with customers and the magnitude of their involvement with service delivery.

Figure 32: Employee customer interactions*

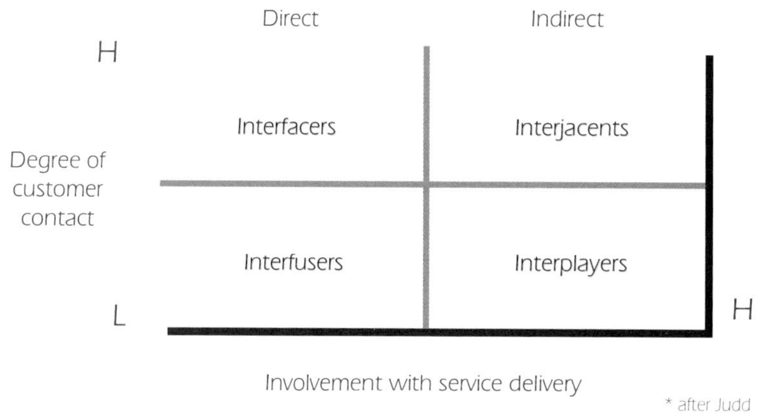

Understanding each role allows us to understand where they add value (or might destroy it!).

Interfacers: frequent or extensive periods of contact with customers and heavily involved in delivery of services.

Interjacents: staff such as receptionists or telephone operators – constant involvement but little delivery – often first point of contact however.

Interfusers: often involved in development of services but little involvement in delivery – e.g. strategic managers, marketing, research – must develop customer awareness by giving them the opportunity to understand customer interactions.

Interplayers: support staff who have little contact with customers and only indirect involvement in service delivery.

Measures need to be developed taking into account each type of role to ensure their activities add value and they are motivated and rewarded accordingly. In addition there will be different training needs for each type of role.

'We've finally come to realize that its not bricks and mortar; all you have is people'

Ted McDowell, *Toronto Dominion*

Processes

Most processes have evolved over time and were not designed into their current state. Where previous improvements took place, if any, they were focused within functions and, therefore, contributed to the fragmented nature of operations. This has been compounded by computerization that generally tended to concentrate on mechanising the existing activities which resulted in extra, unnecessary steps and many steps still carried out but rendered meaningless. They are often full of significant duplication and double checking and opportunities for value to be added to the customer are countered by activities which add no value. Usually they take poor cognisance of true customer needs.

There is, therefore, great improvement potential and moving to Customer Relationship Management demands that this is done in order to offer the right service cost-effectively to your customers. What this means is that you change to customer-driven processes:

- think of things from the customers' perspective (he or she doesn't want a product (mortgage/loan); he or she wants to buy a house/vehicle)
- focus on value to customers at the right price and quality (ask what they are thinking)
- use appropriate resources to deliver (people, systems, outsource, joint ventures, partnerships, etc)
- eliminate non-value added activities and overheads
- re-design the processes and then train the staff adequately

The best processes should have:

- minimal handoffs
- minimal logical roles
- a set of common 'rules' that govern execution
- the ability to impute cost onto activities to arrive at costed processes
- well-defined start and end points
- clearly understood inputs, changes and outputs

Systems

Key questions here are:

- Can our existing systems support us going forward – if not what do we need?

- How will they interface with existing systems?

- What should the output be?

- How long will it take to implement new systems?

Basically it will almost certainly require a new set of 'middleware' to run the Customer Relationship Management data analysis and probably systems enhancements to legacy systems to work with the new Customer Relationship Management software (*see* Chapter 12: Customer Relationship Management and IT).

Structure

For Customer Relationship Management to be effective the structure needs to be addressed. This involves the whole way the organization looks at customers. The diagram below shows the key points for consideration in that after the vision and CVP have been agreed and the objectives of Customer Relationship Management then it is necessary to decide if the structure will support it – and if not to change it to one that will.

Figure 33: Focusing effort on the CVP to maximize CRM

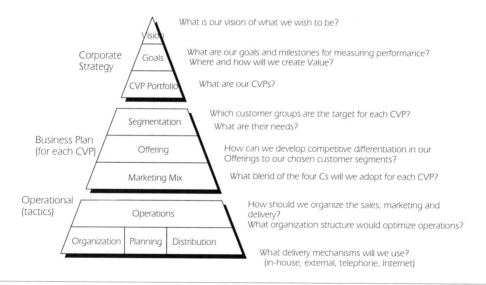

Typical changes to structure that will be required will include:

- delegation of responsibility down to relationship managers for some decisions

- changes to reporting lines depending on the current position

- de-layering to move responsible staff and decision makers closer to customers

- channel changes to streamline customer service

Case study: Postbanken

The Swedish bank Postbanken has opted for a fast-track development. Its CRM strategy includes one statement for all accounts and personal advice.

Ralf Blomquist, managing partner of Customer:view AB, speaking at a recent IFS London seminar, outlined the successful implementation of a CRM strategy at Postbanken in Sweden – a joint venture between Nordea and the Swedish Post Office. The aim of the service was to offer mass market banking under the motto: 'Come as you are'.

Explaining the implementation of Postbanken's CRM strategy, which took only six months, Blomquist said three principal building blocks were considered important for developing a mature system:

● A consolidated view of an account for both the bank and the customer

● Customer-bank dialogue management.

● Opportunity spotting, or lead generation, for the bank and the customer.

To implement the system, Postbanken opted for a fast-track solution to take advantage of the much shorter development time required. Outlining the key features of the customer statement, which included one statement for all accounts, attractive presentation and personal advice based on specific events related to the banking relationship, Blomquist described the results to date as 'outstanding'.

Despite the fact that the bank is less than five years old, he said the bank has '460,000 customers, was profitable from its first year, has the highest scores on customer satisfaction and loyalty in the industry, and has achieved brand recognition well above average expectations'.

Why Customer Relationship Management initiatives fail

Putting Customer Relationship Management in place within an organization is usually a serious undertaking, given the changes that are required. It is a fact, however, that many projects are unsuccessful – or have been hitherto. There are a number of key reasons why Customer Relationship Management initiatives have failed in the past. They include:

● The board has little customer/Customer Relationship Management understanding or involvement

● Rewards and incentives are tied to old, non-customer objectives so staff attitudes remain rooted in old practices

● Staff culture does not have a focus on the customer and is, rather, driven by processes and procedures and hierarchical considerations

- Limited or no input from the customers' perspective – and as a result only the organization's views are taken into account

- Too much focus was placed on 'software as the solution' and, as a result, basic factors such as architecture and integration are forgotten

- Poor quality customer data and information

- Little coordination of multiple departmental initiatives and projects

- Creation of the Customer Relationship Management team is left until too late and often business staff are not involved

- No measures or monitoring of benefits

Usually an organization recognizes a problem and, therefore, decides that the answer is that it needs Customer Relationship Management. More often than not there is no clear understanding of what Customer Relationship Management is, nor what the implications are for an organization. As a result a poorly thought-out and ill-considered piece of analysis is offered up as a business case to the organization's senior executives who have still not answered in their own minds the questions – 'What is Customer Relationship Management?' and 'What will it mean for us?' As a result it is being set up to fail.

Typically for many projects the denouement is:

- A hospital pass of 'implementing Customer Relationship Management' is given to a newly appointed Customer Relationship Management manager

- She quickly puts a team together which has a poor brief.

- Large sums of money are spend on systems and customization.

- Objectives are insufficiently clear

- Timings are unrealistic and unachievable

- The project does not take the users with it so it does not deliver and is not used properly.

Result – frustration, poor customer service – and, if it has been externally communicated to the media, bad press coverage when it becomes clear that it will not deliver.

This can be avoided by simple planning:

A plan ;

- Has objectives that can be measured

- Answers the questions that stakeholders should be asking

- Builds in options and contingencies

- Identifies and quantifies risks and sets out to minimize or quantify them

- Allows progress to be measured

- It is prepared with input from all stakeholders and therefore achieves buy-in to the output and deliverables
- It has a budget and resource allocation to deliver
- It gives :
  - Certainty
  - Measures
  - A route map
  - Confidence
  - Evidence of forethought
- It shapes the thinking
- It considers scenarios and implications and ensures that points have not been missed
- It identifies weaknesses
- It provides a communication tool to the stakeholders within a frame of reference to which they have assented

Figure 34: CRM requires company-wide support

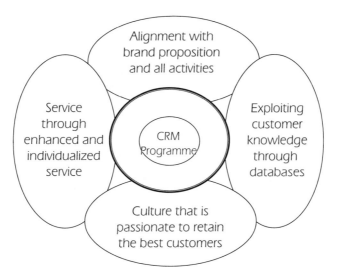

The diagram above shows the key components of a successful Customer Relationship Management programme – it needs company-wide support to ensure that it is aligned with customer and brand strategy; that the culture has been changed to support it; that adequate databases have been developed which allow the information to take the right decisions and manage the customers; and that service permeates the organization.

Key learning points

1. Effective Customer Relationship Management is not a quick fix.

2. Too often insufficient attention is paid to the planning and analysis as well as omitting to obtain organizational buy-in to the project.

3. Planning is key before even starting the programme.

Further reading

Neil Russell-Jones: *Managing Change Pocketbook*

Stone and Woodcock: *Relationship Marketing*

Summary

In this section the basic foundations of Customer Relationship Management have been considered. The next section – Developing a Customer Relationship Initiative – will consider how to establish Customer Relationship Management within your organization and the steps that must be followed.

II

Developing a Customer Relationship Management Initiative

8

UNDERSTANDING CUSTOMERS

Topics in this chapter

- Buying behaviour
- Delivery differentiation
- Features v. Benefits
- Customer Value Proposition
- Selling

Syllabus topics covered

- Consumer behaviour principles.
- Organizational buying behaviour.
- Retail and business customer profiling.
- Relationship life cycles.
- Understanding and managing customer expectations.
- Building relationships by adding value to customers cost effectively.
- Effective interviews with customers.

Introduction

Understanding customers is very different, at the micro level, from knowing your customer. It is about understanding the propensities of a set of customers (see segmentation) to purchase services and what they will pay for them. The key components are:

Customer value

Customer behaviour

Customer satisfaction

These three items are closely linked and by taking all three into consideration when managing your clients the better the result will be for you. It is impossible to consider only one in isolation – at least it is not possible so to do effectively.

Customer Relationship Management is about developing a set of performance metrics that enable you to measure these three items, conduct gap analysis, develop actions to close the gaps (for those customers that will generate value) and manage the customers to improve performance.

Satisfaction is an intangible but can have a major effect on your business. Highly satisfied customers on average are five times more likely to stay with your organization than those that are merely satisfied. Dissatisfied customers, however, tell others and it is estimated that they tell over 10 others! Moreover only about 5% complain – so for every customer complaint that you hear about another 20 have had similar experiences. Resolving a complaint satisfactorily, however, has a very beneficial effect on the customer's perception of the organization and as a result tends to increase loyalty.

Figure 35: Understanding customers – key components

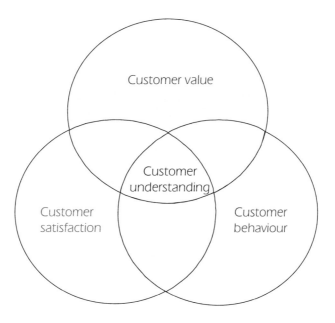

8.1   Customer value

This is the value to your organization of your customers. At the macro level it is revenue less costs and a proportion of losses incurred. At the individual level (lifetime) value can be loosely calculated as:

Value from transactions (product purchase or usage)

times

Number of transactions per year (extrapolated out and averaged)

times

Expected lifetime of relationship (how long either you will be in business or how long you expect realistically your customers to stay with you)

(Discounted down to NPV)

This can be a staggering sum, not only for corporates but also for individuals – particularly when you add in increasing product penetration, referrals (at a representative proportion of value) etc and brings home the message of understanding value.

Worked example 1

Take a large food retailer. A typical customer probably goes in once a week and spends around £100, plus £200 say twice a year at Christmas and for other special occasions. This represents an annual value of around £5,400 per person! Over a ten-year period this would be (at constant values) £54,000. For every customer lost this represents a major disruption to cash flow – and they then have to replace them just to stay still. For every 1,000 customers that they lose the (annualized) value lost is £5.4 million and the lifetime value at constant values is £54 million!

Take a bank. A typical customer might have:

- A mortgage of £150,000 on which you charge interest spread of 1%, plus fees
- A current account with charges of £100 pa – plus free cash
- A £10,000 loan for a car which earns you 2.5%

There may also be potential to sell them

- A life policy
- Buildings and contents insurance
- F/X through you as well as travellers cheques say twice a year
- Credit card

By adding all these up for your own organization, even an ordinary customer is of great benefit to the organization, and when annualized this value is even greater!

However, the lifetime value is of even greater importance when you consider the real benefits from Customer Relationship Management. A small increase in retention has a massively disproportionate effect on the lifetime value of a client. This is because the embedded value increases geometrically the longer that they stay.

For example, in personal insurance changing the retention rate from say 90% to 95% increases the customer lifetime value by a staggering 84%!! This is because with an average retention rate of 90% the customer stays on average 10 years but with 95% retention rate the average loyalty is 20 years![11]

Figure 36: Increasing the customer lifetime value by retention

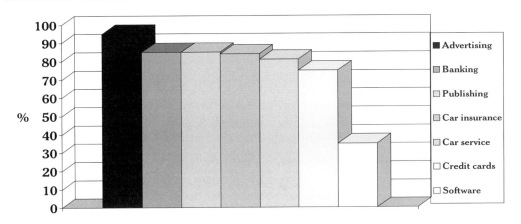

How much (%) a 5% retention in value lifts lifetime value

The effects of increased retention rates are, therefore, spectacular. The objective of Customer Relationship Management is of course to effect this increase in loyalty and, therefore, value to the business.

Case study[12]

An insurance company with 90% retention

Has	100,000 customers
Average customer lifetime value	£280
Business value	£28 million

But if it can increase its average retention to 95% it will

Have	155,000 customers
Average customer lifetime value	£515
Business value	£80 million

[11] Frederick F Reichheld: *The Loyalty Effect* (Harvard Business School Press 1996)
[12] Peter Doyle: *Value-Based Marketing* (Wiley 2000)

It not only gains a net 55,000 customers as it has reduced its customer loss but they will now stay for 20 years instead of 10 (so doubling business) but in addition, due to the longevity of embedded value, they increase their value by over 80% to £515.

As a result business value virtually trebles!

It is, therefore, extremely important both to:

- maximize value from customers;

- maximize retention; and

- minimize the number of customers who are likely to deliver low value (or losses).

Customer behaviour

This is the way in which a customer 'doles out' his share of wallet or 'spend'. Does he put all his transactions through you? Or does he multi-bank (a more common phenomenon than hitherto)? If he has a life policy – do you also have mortgage protection policy, buildings and contents, or perhaps car and other insurance from him? Or is it spread across several companies (quite likely – especially if the lender for his mortgage has sold policies)? If the latter two situations are the case – why is this and what can you do to change it or influence him to reconsider – next time? Clearly the more that you can influence him to put through you – the greater his lifetime value will be.

Customer satisfaction

What determines how much share of wallet you receive is largely the level of satisfaction that the customer in turn receives from you. Satisfied customers are the ones that continue to take your products and services. It is worth noting that just satisfying them is insufficient, because it will take only a marginally more attractive offer to entice them away – a better Customer Value Proposition. Note that for *very* dissatisfied customers they may leave even with a worse offer!!

Case study: Thomsons

Thomson the holiday company offer package tours to millions in many destinations.

Package tours invariably involve issues of a multi-varied nature (poor hotel service, late transfers, late flights, trips that were not what was expected etc.) The resort staff, however, are used to dealing with crises. The staff are trained to sort out problems in situ and to make recompense immediately wherever possible. For major issues then they send compensation to the customers' home address so that it is waiting for them when they arrive home from their holiday. This creates a very favourable impression with customers and they have great loyalty from their customers with many repeat bookings. Many customers are paying for holidays up to a year in advance so it is vital that they are managed properly – the cash flow implications would be disastrous. Thomson takes customer loyalty and lifetime value seriously.

People will trade much for convenience *as they see it* and if you are only just satisfying them they will switch to somewhere else – often on a whim.

Customer Relationship Management is about ensuring that your customers are **very** satisfied – or it is about finding out **why** they are not and *doing something about it*! This influences their behaviour so that you maintain customer value.

Figure 37: High benefits usually imply high delivery costs

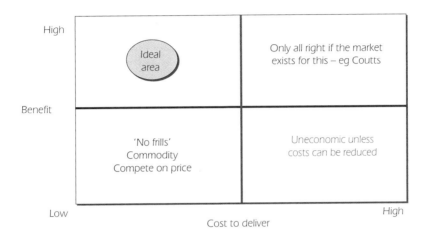

What does a customer want? What does it cost to deliver?
And how much will they pay?

It is equally important that you understand the cost to the organization of delivering that value. Where there is high benefit there is almost always a high cost of delivery. You must ensure that if you are in this market then the income you receive reflects this higher cost – otherwise you will be subsidising your customers very handsomely. The ideal area is where you deliver high benefit at low cost. Unfortunately there are not many areas like that.

If the value delivered costs more to deliver than the income received – then it begs the question as to why you are offering this level of service. Could you offer a lower level of service and a cheaper cost – or can you charge more for the premium service you are offering?

Offerings vis-à-vis competition and core competencies

To sell your services/products you must be sure that what you are offering is based around your core competencies. Where customers do not perceive that your offering is a core competency then it will be that much harder to persuade them to take it. The competition will be well entrenched in the customers' minds and very hard to dislodge. By basing what you offer around the core competencies – and understanding where that gives you competitive advantage – you should be better placed to persuade them to take your products. For example, it would be very hard for a regional building society to break into the corporate treasury market. No-one would believe that it had the experience nor anything else to offer above the competition. However, it would be relatively easy to move into property financing because it would have plenty of experience (albeit in the retail market) on which it could build. The key issues here are the flexibility across your offerings that your core competencies offer and the difficulty of competitors replicating it. The diagram below shows this and the competitive responses that you need to make. For financial services generally the products are easily replicable and, therefore, it is how you differentiate yourself that matters in most cases.

Figure 38: Core competencies – related to offerings

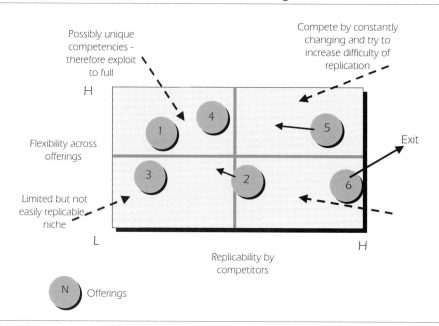

8.2　Why do customers buy?

Customers buy because they have (or believe that they have) a need for something. These needs lie at several levels and are known as Maslow's 'Hierarchy of needs' (hygiene, safety, social, esteem and self-actualization[13]). The need that drives them to buy something may be at a low level such as a 'hygiene' factor (food, shelter, heat etc) or something more esoteric – I need a holiday (esteem), or I want to buy a new DVD player (social/self-actualization). Recognition of this need drives them to action to meet the need.

Often wants are mixed up with needs:

- eg I **want** a Rolls Royce or a Ferrari or an Aston Martin

[13] Abraham Maslow: *Motivation and Personality* (Harper & Row 1970)

- but I really **need** a car
- or do I **need** some form of transport
- or do I really just **want** a status symbol for other people to see
- or am I so rich and bored that I don't know what I **need or want?**

(*See* Needs and Wants Chapter x.)

They then enter into a process to meet this need. They will not of course follow this course of action consciously but more likely post-rationalize a decision or merely act on instinct (food) or even habit – there is no real need to eat at set times of the day – breakfast or lunch time – it is just a generally accepted thing.

The path is as follows (generic):

E **existence** of a need (eg food) not recognized

R **realization** that the need exists (he feels hungry)

A understanding that something must be done about it **(action)**

S information **search** (where can I buy/get food?)

E **evaluation** the information (how far, how much, how expensive, type)

S **selection** of some food (and consumption) and thereby

ERASES the need.

Needs can be:

- immediate (eat now)
- repetitive (eat everyday)
- deferrable (change house)
- long term (buy house)
- cyclical (change car).

Sometimes things occur to change this perception of need:

- a woman gets married and takes out life insurance and mortgage protection
- A man gets divorced and cancels joint accounts
- A baby is born and his parents open a savings account
- A woman inherits a house and sells her own and liquidates the mortgage and the protection policy

There are also several different types of purchase – notwithstanding the needs:

Brand new – no experience of the product or service, the customer will need a lot of data and you are trying to sell the product and establish a relationship at the same time. Eg an undergraduate opening an account for the first time or a young person thinking about taking out life cover (a very hard sell – known in the trade as 'immortals').

Replacement – routine, taking the same as before eg re-booking your skiing chalet at the end of your skiing week, or rolling over an overdraft, or annual house/car insurance. (When engaging a decorator or builder it is common to obtain at least three quotes. Thereafter, if service was good it is common to use the same one next time.)

Customer Relationship Management has a key role to play in ensuring that the rollover is as smooth as possible and this opportunity is not lost due a silly error, and to fight off potential competition. Customer Relationship Management can also be used to facilitate product penetration by offering complementary or relevant products and services at the rollover.

Referral – where the customer has been recommended to you by an existing customer. You do not have a relationship but you must build on the existing relationship with the referee and take that into account – can be tricky sometimes, for example if the new customer does not fulfil criteria.

Substitution – where the customer is replacing the previous purchase but with a different offering. This is, therefore, a combination of brand new and replacement. You are trying to establish the relationship, but they have the experience of previous purchases (and if it is a similar replacement – presumably a bad service) or perhaps a change of circumstance (up-grade from a Fiesta to, say, a Mercedes E class).

Figure 39: Who really thinks about it?

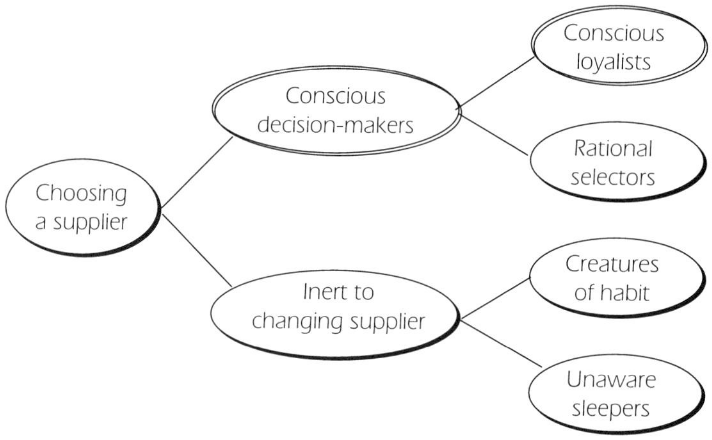

Decisions of course are not always taken in the right way or in the right frame of mind. Many are not thought about at all. The diagram above considers someone thinking about changing a supplier. There are two basic premises – that they are consciously thinking about it or are not thinking about it at all. This leads to there being four states:

Unaware sleepers – who have no conscious input at all.

Creatures of habit – who think about it but prefer the known to the unknown. Much advertising is aimed at making people switch brands or suppliers because it is a well-known fact that inertia is a powerful factor in your favour as a supplier. People do not change unless there is a stimulus for it, but once having changed they adopt the new supplier or way of doing things as a habit – especially where they cannot go back.

Conscious loyalists – those who think about decisions but consciously and deliberately decide to stay with the 'devil that they know'.

Rational selectors – people who will always take a rational view of what they are doing and will always open the field up to others – good for those struggling to gain a foot hold in a company – less good for those established suppliers.

Clearly the best customer base consists of conscious loyalists and creatures of habit.

8.3 Buying behaviour

Customers typically take into account a wide variety of buying factors, including:

- specific product features and benefits
- support services provided, such as technical advice
- product/service availability
- company image
- delivery arrangements/packaging
- price per unit, total cost and 'value'...

...and different customer groups may have different needs and priorities. You must, therefore, understand the key factors for target segments and then optimize the Customer Value Proposition to maximize market share.

Figure 40: Customers buy for different reasons

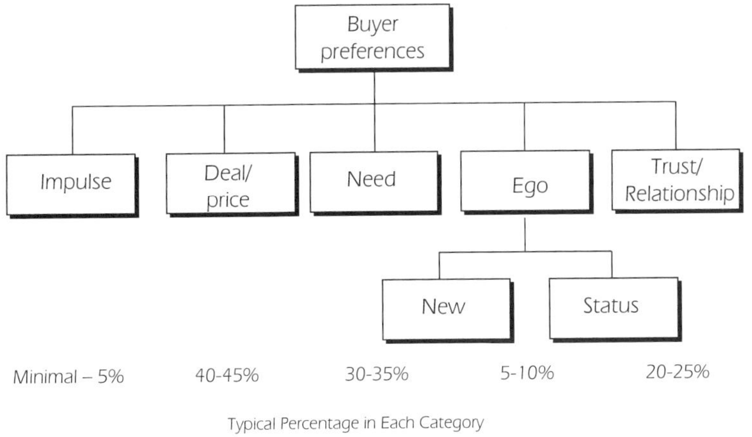
Buyer preferences
Impulse
Deal/ price
Need
Ego
Trust/ Relationship
New
Status
Minimal – 5%
40-45%
30-35%
5-10%
20-25%
Typical Percentage in Each Category

The key question is 'What drives their preference?'

Customers buy for different reasons based on the drivers behind the decision. A purchase may be based on a combination of several drivers but analysis has shown that typically they fall into five broad categories:

- **Impulse** – where they are taken by the moment and suddenly buy something. Sometimes known as stress purchases. Eg you are travelling a long way in a car and you stop to buy food or a CD to play because you have forgotten your own. You will buy something that is there – even if it is not your best preference – you will choose the one that you consider you will have least cause to 'regret'.

- **Deal/price** – usually a commodity purchase where no extra value is perceived or where the purchaser likes the thrill of 'doing a deal' and demonstrating the bargain he drove based on his competence.

- **Need** – a major driver – *see* Needs and Wants.

- **Ego** – where the purchase will in his view give him credibility in his peer group or the world at large. Could be:

  - **New products or services** – early adopters like to be seen with the latest gizmo or service to impress

  - **Status** – by buying something they believe will give them referent charisma from owning the service or product

- **Trust/relationship** – where they buy based on the trust that they have in the vendor.

Each purchase will be made up of a combination of these five areas but the emphasis will be different for each person and may exclude one or more areas (preference 0%). Understanding these drivers is crucial to selling to customers. Customer Relationship Management provides the understanding of these drivers and enables you to sell the right products to customers by meeting these drivers and demonstrating the benefits in your customers' terms of perception.

Customer input to the purchase

This varies from decision to decision. Some purchasing decisions are very easy (buy a sandwich) and, although they involve choice, represent a very low 'risk' and will yield insignificant 'regret' if the decision goes wrong. Most purchases are of commodities (by volume not necessarily by value) such as bread, milk, petrol, etc. Little heed is paid to the brand in most circumstances and it is the price/convenience trade-off that is the primary factor. Look at the success of 'white branded goods' in supermarkets.

As a result, therefore, customers put little, or no, effort into these purchases; and they have little or no compunction in changing should circumstances demand or facilitate it and it suits them. For example, most people fill up with petrol when their petrol tanks are nearly empty and accordingly use the nearest petrol outlet – or when it is convenient – say at a visit to a supermarket or a motorway restaurant – and could not probably tell you which brand of petrol they purchased even if you asked them immediately afterwards. Brand, therefore, plays little or no part in the purchasing decision.

Where their need is a major one (car or house purchase) or is perceived to be important (clothes and goods that reflect style) the customer is more likely to devote a great deal of effort into the purchase. This is particularly so where goods have a high degree of 'visibility' (cars, clothes, music, furniture and may include other items such as credit cards or cheque accounts).

This reflects the **risk/regret** trade-off. What is the **risk** to me of doing this – in terms of price, people's views of me; and what will my level of **regret** be if I do not make the purchase – if I don't buy a house I have to pay rent which I might regard as dead money, whereas if I buy a house I have to service the mortgage and everything else that comes with it and represents a higher risk to me, but I obtain (ceteris paribus) capital appreciation and I might regret that benefit if I rented. Equally if I fail to insure my home against risks (fire, subsidence, flood, theft etc) and something happens I will be hit badly potentially and, therefore, will regret it very much.

These types of purchases have a high degree of effort and input/involvement from customers and are, therefore, important in the context of Customer Relationship Management. By exercising good management when there is high input from the customers you can considerably influence decisions and also increase customer loyalty because you are seen to be helping them with a difficult or risky decision and they will appreciate it, and will have confidence in future subsequent transactions within the relationship. Conversely poor management here will conceivably turn them off you for life.

8.4   Branding

Branding is very important to Customer Relationship Management. It is not, however, about TV adverts – or at least not solely – but it is about how customers are handled at the sharp end. All the adverts in the world will not bring a customer back if she feels that she was handled badly or that she had a very bad experience with one part of the organization that outweighed the many other favourable transactions/interactions. In her mind the brand is now damaged goods.

Branding campaigns establish the name of an organization or its service features in the customers' minds, but it is in the direct encounters that it is characterized and subsequently the perception is crystallized. Branding can make goods 'must have', eg 'Cabbage Patch Kids' in the USA in the 80s, or 'Hermes scarves' where the cachet from owning one and being associated with the brand is enormous and wearing one is virtually 'de rigueur' for mothers picking up children from independent schools in the UK.

In recent years the branding that has accompanied television series or films has resulted in huge merchandising of basic ordinary goods. Eg 'Thunderbirds' toys such as 'Tracy Island' models; Harry Potter mugs which are just ordinary mugs with a picture on the front; or dinosaur-branded fast food where the paper plates and cups have a picture of a dinosaur which is nothing to do with anything in particular but is cashing on the increased desire for dinosaur-related goods following on from the success of the film *Jurassic Park*.

Another excellent example of this in a generic sense is the recent explosion in demand for 4 x 4 cars in London and the Home Counties and other major cities and towns. This is despite the fact that they are uneconomical, fairly unsuited to the driving in busy cities (on-road) and difficult to park – but because they are currently the height of fashion.

Branding is, however, ephemeral – as anyone who invested in Dot.com shares is only too aware and brands can disappear ('Victory V' cough sweets, 'Glees') or even worse become associated with bad events – eg Barclays took a lot of unfair publicity over a sensible business decision to close unprofitable branches and it damaged the brand in some people's eyes.

Case study: Marlboro

Marlboro is a major cigarette producer in the USA and had traditionally always sold on the cachet of better quality and, therefore, the cigarettes were higher priced. On the back of this they sold a lot of associated merchandise (clothing etc) and it had a very good stock price reflecting the premium cash flows thereby generated. A competitor aggressively attacked the market offering cheap cigarettes and started to hurt Marlboro's share. The response by Marlboro was to reduce prices – a staggering response for a premium product and something that the board had always stated that they would never do. As a result the perception changed into 'just another cigarette' and without the cachet price became a driving factor – customers accordingly switched to other brands. The result – on what has become known as Marlboro Monday – was a dramatic fall in the stock price and an alteration in perception of the brand overnight. It took a long and difficult campaign to re-establish itself as a premium brand.

This response was taken with inadequate regard for the consequences of damaging customers' perception of the brand and with a misunderstanding of the terms on which the Customer Value Proposition had been formulated – in this case **Product/Customers needs and wants** not **Price/Cost** – with dire results.

Contrast that approach to the response to a similar threat to competition by Heublein:

Case study: Heublein

Smirnoff was the leading brand of vodka in the USA. A competitor of Heublein, which makes Smirnoff, attacked this position by selling a vodka at a lower price while claiming it was the same quality. This started to hurt Heublein's share and the management had to respond to this threat.

The response was very considered and contained several elements which demonstrated a good understanding of branding and buying perceptions. It would have been easy to match the reduced price but that would have resulted in reduced profits and probably a price war, as well as destroying the perception of Smirnoff as a premium brand (*vide* Marlboro). Instead the company ***increased*** the price of Smirnoff and introduced another brand – Relska – to compete with the competitor's new brand.

They further compounded the defensive response by introducing a *third* brand – Popov – priced lower than Relska to sweep up those that bought on price. The result confirmed Smirnoff as the premium brand and the competitor came to be regarded as just another vodka. Profits increased handsomely. All three brands are of course virtually indistinguishable in taste and also in manufacturing costs – but customer perception when purchasing is all.

How services are delivered is of critical importance to customers and the type of service they receive shapes this. The more complex the offering the greater and more intense the type of help or service a customer requires.

Most clients are pretty familiar with most products in a general sense but there are occasions when the service is complex (or new) and at other times they require specific customization. The diagram below shows this and breaks the type of service required down onto four quadrants which of course have differential pricing requirements. It shows how best to manage customers expectations by offering different types of service:

Expertise/modular

This is where you are offering a fairly complex product with a low degree of customization. You therefore need to explain the product to a customer but do not need to develop or enhance it to accommodate their needs. He is paying for your expertise in having already developed the product and in helping him to understand it.

Figure 41: Delivery differentiation – customers' perception

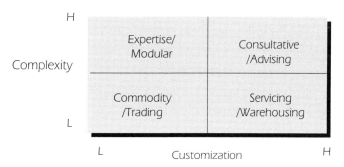

What the customer gets is a combination of experience of the product and the level of customization – affects the price (CVP trade-off)

Commodity/trading

Where the product is simple and so too is the level of customization – eg current accounts or credit cards, or term assurance. This is a commodity purchase and sales will typically be predicated on price.

Servicing/warehousing

The product is not complex but it needs customizing for the client. Here you are adding value by making it fit his particular needs. Typically it might contain a blend of several ordinary products to match requirements. Charging is a combination of product pricing and service. You might take an ordinary letter of credit, link it with a performance guarantee, a stand-by facility and a F/X contract to deliver financing for a particular product. You might also join with another supplier to provide the necessary product.

Consultative advising

In this case typically the product does not exist and has to be developed. Both are in uncertain territory and you are to a certain extent advising the customer on what he might need. It is important to put the risk with the customer, as this is a very complex area and therefore out of the norm of usual products. Pricing will reflect this. Good examples would be special hedge instruments or derivatives created especially for a customer.

The key issue here is that the customers' perception of the type of delivery will affect how he views the service and – perhaps more importantly – what he will pay for it.

Customers will usually pay premium prices for consultative/advisory services rather than commodity delivery – which is just as well because as complexity and customization increases so too does the cost of delivering it and therefore the price that customers should pay.

8.5 Understanding the customer

It is vital that you understand the customer in the context within which he is situated.

For a personal customer this includes:

- Lifestyle
- Place of work
- Type of work
- Income
- Future expectations
- Family status
- Residence

For a corporate this includes:

- The economy in which they operate

- Legislation

- Competition

- Environmental considerations

- Technology

- Culture

- Finance

- Operations

- Sector-specific issues

- Local/geographic issues

- Politics

…all tempered by the legislation that affects what you can do. Financial services is very heavily regulated and subject to all manner of legal and other restraints, which also need to be understood – eg capital adequacy, money laundering, best practice, best advice etc.

There is also a key difference between personal and corporates:

the latter too have customers.

If you can understand what they need to do for their customers and assist them in this aspect you will go a long way towards giving them a service that is better than the competition and helps them to help *their* customers.

By working with your customer to help him improve what he does for his customers you are forging a much tighter bond with him, increasing his loyalty and making it that much harder for the competition to take him away. A likely outcome is that he may introduce you to his customer as well – as he moves towards being a supporter. For example in some letters of credit there are provisions for pre-payments to the customers' customer to assist them in preparing the goods for export.

The diagram overleaf shows this and the key area of focus is to meet all three needs – yours, your customer's and his customers' needs.

Figure 42: Improve your customer's life

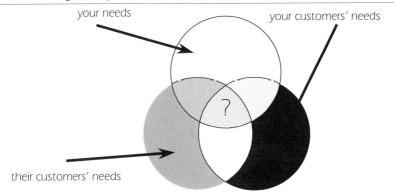

What can you do to improve his day and his customer's day?

The more that you can place your offerings in the centre box (**'?'**) then the greater help that you will be giving to your customer. By helping them to satisfy their customers' needs you are making them feel that you are in partnership with them and progressively moving them up the ladder of satisfaction.

Exploding myths

All organizations are full of myths and folklore about customers. These will influence behaviour of staff to meet perceived customers and often result in initiatives that are wholly wrong. It is best to tackle these head-on and disprove them so as to ensure that behaviour is correct and customer-focused.

Case study: Insurance company

An insurance company that sold only life products through a self-employed direct sales force was convinced, despite general sector analysis to the contrary, that its customer base was largely AB, C1. This was in the face of low premiums, and low persistency. Only when a comprehensive analysis of the customer base was carried out and hard evidence presented did management come to see that their client base was largely C2, DE and, therefore, representing much lower value per policy and typically with premiums that were too high to be sustainable and changed their approach (too late unfortunately).

An understanding of your customers is vital in order to target products and effort effectively. It is impossible to sell the products that you wish to sell if you do not understand who your customers are and more importantly what they want.

This must be linked with the benefit that you receive – customers will always take 'free' benefits from you and this incurs a cost. You must evaluate what you are delivering and ensure that it is cost-effective and focused on the areas that will maximize the return.

Where loyalty schemes are established it is vital to understand if they are delivering adequate value back and that the right customers benefit from them – eg frequent-flyer schemes usually award points for distance travelled – which may not necessarily reflect cost and profit to the airline:

Case study: Delta

Delta had an airmiles scheme based on traditional lines – ie distances flown. By matching revenue earned to frequent flyers it noticed that the two were not the same, and in fact a tendency towards an inverse correlation. It, therefore, redeveloped the scheme to reward those flyers that generate revenue and not necessarily those that fly regularly.

Key commandments

- Understand your customer base

- Understand your customers' requirements/business

- Prioritize your customers

- Manage out unpopular customers

- Sell a larger range of products to existing customers

- Target new customers in profitable sectors/segments

- Seek to move into new segments where you can make money

Without customers you have no business and they are not obliged to take your products – therefore, you must sell your products to them. To do this you must set targets:

- For revenue

- To convert leads

- To drum up more leads

- To manage existing customers

Having set the targets you must then align remuneration with the targets to encourage behaviours to change and establish the mechanisms for measuring and monitoring progress.

8.6   Selling

Selling is about 'persuasive communication' – ie that is perceived as adding value to you and your customer. It is therefore vital that you are clear as to what your organization offers.

Figure 43: Optimize your understanding

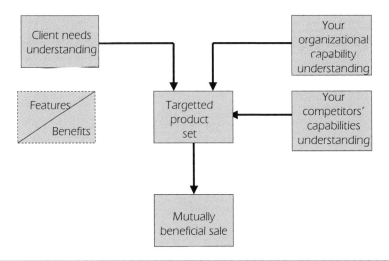

Therefore, you must do your homework. You need to understand for each client:

● the client needs

● your capability in his context

● the competitors' capabilities in his context

and develop a targeted product set that meets his needs, better than the competition, to close a mutually beneficial deal.

Why should the customer buy from you? …rather than the competition? You must translate your products into benefits to the client – eg '…this means that…'

For example, a life policy could equate to 'peace of mind' and generate you better returns than the others from our investment performance; we have an easier claims service; we are flexible on premiums etc.

8.7   Understanding competition

The first step to understanding the competition is to know who they are. They will differ from segment to segment and will not always include the same entities. Eg for you it might include:

● Other high street banks

● Building societies

● Insurance companies

● e-banks

● direct telesales banks

- finance houses
- corporates
- overseas entities
- foreign banks in the UK

...they are usually selling similar things which represents both an issue (how to differentiate) as well as an opportunity (your differential).

You also need to understand where you are in the 'price band'. If your offering is out of its perceived price band then the customers will have a false impression of the value that they might expect versus the price they might expect to pay.

Putting an offering often requires inputs from across the whole organization. Too often strategies are based around a business unit – or part of one when in fact it is offerings that compete in the marketplace – and this usually involves parts of the organization that are outside your own part. For example, a branch may need specialist input from its international arm, its investment management unit or its corporate or treasury to put a package of offerings together for a client.

Figure 44: Strategy v. Organization structure

Many organizations are split into Head offices and profit centres.

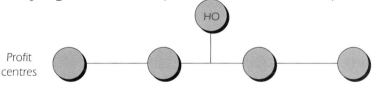

This is a **Financial** model not a **strategic market-facing** model. A competitive model represents an organization and its offerings are more likely to correlate in a **matrix**.

Profit centre managers manage resources. Offerings may coincide (E/5), or more likely cut across several. Too often competitive strategies are developed by profit centres (internally focused) not offerings (client centric) and, therefore, fail.

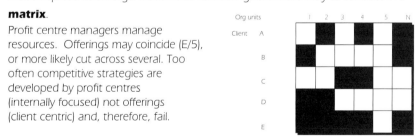

8.8   The corporate buying cycle

Dealing with corporate customers is very different from dealing with individuals. Selling a corporate your services presents a many-faceted problem for the following reasons:

- Corporates are not people and so respond in different ways – they have cultures, their own ways of doing things and are composed of many people

- They contain (often) many different departments and divisions with different goals

- Their staff are all different and will respond differently to the same stimuli

- They often have different delegated levels of discretion which means that decisions are frequently taken by:

  - different people

  - at different levels within the organization

  - in different ways

- Frequently there is a central control imposed in all or some aspects (eg many companies have a central treasury department that looks after much of its financial services needs) or more commonly central purchasing policies (eg we use this bank, this software, this travel company or this insurance company only)

- They are often in many locations within a country (eg major UK retailers such as Tesco, Marks and Spencer, Sainsburys) and in banking Abbey National Lloyds/TSB, Halifax; frequently they operate internationally – across two or more countries (Walmart/ASDA, Carrefour, Barclays, BBVA, Banco do Brasil, CGNU, Willis Coroon) or globally (Shell, BP, McDonald's, Citibank)

- They may be subsidiaries of foreign companies and, therefore, subject to different rules and regulations and with an overseas head or regional office where many decisions are taken

There are other reasons if you think about this, but suffice to say that dealing with corporates is much more difficult than with individuals.

It is, therefore, of critical importance to understand the corporate buying process within an organization. This is part of understanding your customer but it is so important that if this aspect is overlooked it becomes virtually impossible to deal successfully with corporates. To this end you must find and then cultivate the real decision makers within an organization. This is not as easy as it sounds. Most organizations have a defined decision chain which may be loose or very tight. The key question is 'Where to enter this chain?' and then of course 'How?'

8.9   Getting to maybe

It is very difficult to obtain appointments when calling cold and it is also becoming increasingly difficult to obtain them when they are referred or warm, because people are wary of anyone perceived as 'selling' them something and are busy. Part of the issue as well is that many people do not prepare for the attempt at getting a meeting and so either fail or only partly achieve their goals, thus assisting in reinforcing customers' perception of the pointless appointment for 'selling'.

It is not good enough just to ask for an appointment although many people still try this approach. In simple terms think of the Customer Value Proposition – what is in it for the customer? There must be some benefit to him or her for giving up his or her time and listening (the price) in order for him or her to say yes.

It is very important to let her know both what your objective is and what he or she will gain. A good technique is to put yourself in his or her place and ask – why would I say yes?

For example you might wish to say:

> *'I will be in your area next week and thought you might like to hear about a new product that we have developed especially for your sector (new customer)'*

Or

> *'It is time for the semi-annual review of services (existing customer) and I would like to start the process'*

Or

> *'I would like to introduce a new colleague with some specialist skills that may be of assistance (eg Middle East Energy if that is an area where the organization is interested)'*

What you are striving to do is develop a 'business to business' relationship that transcends the more usual 'buyer to seller' relationship.

There are several factors which pull customers in different ways (real or perceived):

- Time pressure
- Resource constraints
- Internal pressures
- Sales targets which impose worries
- His own customers relationships to manage

Authority is ephemeral

Many staff within corporates are unwilling to admit how little authority they really have. Some of course are very happy to help you to find the right levels in the decision chain – but many do not wish to expose themselves and will not. As a result you can be stuck with your first contact who can be at the wrong level entirely and much time can be wasted in influencing the wrong person.

Typical sales theory focuses on the main types of customer contacts. Note that one person can be part of one group, all of one group and also be in several groups depending on the type of decision, the size of the organization and the importance of the decision:

- **Users** – the person with the need or the person delegated by the organization to fulfil the need. Eg the person to whom responses to an Invitation to Tender must be sent or the manager of the division that needs the facility. They can also be decision-makers and budget holders but often sadly this is not the case, and it is also necessary to cultivate others.

- **Decision-maker** – the person or persons who actually makes the decision to go ahead with something – note that it may be formal or informal authority and ex-officio or *de facto*.

- **Buyers** – those that have the formal authority to agree to a decision to purchase – they are often the same in more routine or low-value decisions.

- **Budget holder** – the person who has the money to pay for your service. May not be the buyer – often is the decision-maker.

- **Coach** – a friend within the organization who, while not necessarily a party to the decision, gives useful information and advice.

- **Influencer** – someone to whom others in the buying process will listen and, therefore, whom you must have on your side. Note that in some circumstances surprising people can be influencers – eg with items such as photocopiers and faxes and often travel it is often people such as administrators who are key.

- **Gate-keeper** – someone who blocks access to others – may be your initial contact who is trying to keep the relationship at that level, an agent who wishes to keep control of the buyer, technical personnel, or often a secretary or someone working closely with someone who refuses to let you get to a customer.

Having established which players are in which category you can then go on to sell services and products.

8.10 The decision cycle

The cycle for a sale is not simple and involves several steps. These steps may take place over quite some elapsed time and in the case of corporates are quite likely to involve several meetings.

Key steps
- Building a relationship and establishing rapport
- Making the opening statement
- Diagnosing the real issues
- Presenting solutions to the issues
- Handling any objections to the solutions

- Closing the sale

- Follow up

They need to be followed in order and the right level of effort put into them. Clearly this will differ depending on what you are selling and to whom but the process does not vary.

Building a relationship and establishing rapport

Objectives here are to break any tension barrier, relax the client, relax yourself and begin to analyse the characteristics of the buyer. For corporates this is often a group of people who have different vested interests in the outcome. Often you have to seek for the hidden questions underpinning their apparent questions. Some examples include:

- '...are you good enough for me to give you my business?'

- '...do you care about me or my business for me to buy from you?'

- '…will you give me the facts that will enable me to make the right decision?'

Making the opening statement

Objectives are to establish your credibility and fitness for what is under discussion (loan, insurance, investment etc), to broaden and deepen the customer's understanding of what you can offer, to focus the meeting on the point at issue and to commence the understanding of the client. The customer will be looking for facts about you and your organization and what differentiates you from the competition.

Diagnosing the real issues

Objectives are to learn more about the client's business and issues, to understand where the individual(s) fit in with the structure and organization – and what their goals are, to understand the real need and to start to look at the decision-making process.

This is usually achieved by questioning the client, and narrowing the focus of the questions progressively until you arrive at your end point. Examples include:

- general remarks to break tension and try to establish some common interest

- questions on the organization and where it is going

- the implications of this and needs arising

- where the individual fits in with the hierarchy and structure

- the customer's needs in that context

- what the opportunity is that arises by meeting these two areas of need

- what the value is therefrom

Presenting solutions to the issues

Objectives are to offer something that meets the customer's needs – eg an overdraft facility linked to working capital finance, trade assistance via letter of credit/trade advances etc, corporate insurance etc – to demonstrate how you will provide the solution eg as a single limit; as several limits greater than the whole within a smaller global solution; several facilities within an overall limit, or insurance for each office discounted down for multi-locations; and to gain agreement to the solution that meets the needs.

Many firms make the mistake of mixing up products with offerings – they are not the same – or not necessarily so. It is how what you offer meets the need or resolves the issue that is important – not the inherent contents. It is important to present the offering in terms of the **benefits** to him and the organization and not to talk of features or products.

There are some key criteria that will affect how a customer makes decisions:

- How your capability is viewed by the organization. This will be in comparison with what they are expecting and against others either currently competing or from past experiences.

- What your experience is of the service you are offering – and where else it has worked successfully.

- The service that supports your offering.

- Timing – when can it happen – duration and flexibility etc.

- What the competition is and how you and your offering compare.

- The cost/benefit trade-off (the Customer Value Proposition).

- Your relationship with the customer.

Above all you must be clear as to the real need and that you can offer a solution.

Handling any objections to the solutions

In an ideal world you present the solution and the customer agrees at once and signs up on the spot. Unfortunately this is rarely the case and at the very least you will get questions of the 'what if' category. It is important that these questions are heard, understood and reacted to otherwise you will not have agreement and the customer will not accept your offering. Therefore, objectives are to refine the solution to meet objections or concerns or variations; to uncover opportunities that you may have missed – '…does it also cover x?; identify the real as opposed to the *prima facie* objection and deal with it; to establish the timescales and agree next steps.

When people object it is not always straightforward to understand why. Sometimes they may say that it does not meet my needs because of 'X' and 'Y'. More often they will vacillate. There are several types of objections:

- **Procrastination** – they try to put the decision off until a later – and often unspecified time; this is very common. You need to clarify the reason for putting the decision off – this usually means that there is another objection – eg they do not have the power to take the decision or that they have not yet obtained agreement to the budget. This needs to be explored, and sorted out.

- **Doubt** – they do no think that you can deliver either the service or part of it or in the time required. You need to clarify this eg by asking a closed question and then rebut the assumption (if you can of course). If there is something that you cannot deliver then come clean – do not lie – customers really get upset about that (quite rightly) and being honest usually pays great dividends as your relationship grows and deepens.

- **Misunderstanding** – real or imagined – about what you offer, the offering or the company. Clarify what it is that is misunderstood and then correct the situation by offering proof or further statements.

- **Indifference** – do not see the need – or do not see the solution. Clarify why they cannot see it and then reiterate a solution to the issues.

- **Real objection** – eg price or you have not offered a service that they require, or there is something that they do not like. This can be a tricky one – especially if you cannot deal with it immediately. Try to place it in context with the other benefits and offerings and offer to sort it out later on.

Generally with objections it is important to prepare for the meeting by putting yourself in the customer's shoes and trying to raise objections and then derive solutions/answers. At all times try to clarify the situation and apologise for not making it clear if this is the case. Control your own emotions – even if you have covered the issue more than once. Ensure that the client agrees that the issue has been resolved satisfactorily.

Closing the sale

This is where you try to close the sale and obtain the customer's agreement. There are two types of close:

- **Assumptive** – where you begin transferring ownership of the offering – '…so we've agreed that you require an overdraft for £x m – when will you draw down your first tranche?'

- **Presumptive** – which is a stronger statement.

And the closes can be:

- **Direct** – '…are you going to agree to this offering (OD, policy etc)?'

- **Choice based** – '…shall I put the facility in place today or next week?'

- **Logical restatement** – '…on balance then this is the logical choice for you…'

Follow up

This is a vital part of the cycle and critical to Customer Relationship Management. Objectives here are to ensure that all is well; to fix any errors; and to seek new or further opportunities. There are two types of follow up – where you have been successful and where you have failed:

Failure

- Try to agree when/if you should make a further visit/arrange a meeting
- Send a follow-up letter promptly
- Execute any interim commitments
- Try to monitor the decision cycle and status and indicate readiness to open discussions again

Success

- Obtain written commitment/signed agreement
- Send contract if necessary
- Agree timings and starting arrangements
- Put in hand necessary actions
- Ensure customer adherence to terms precedent and subsequent as necessary
- Monitor and problem solve
- Arrange reviews etc

Key learning points

1. Lifetime value is of immense importance in deciding which customers are profitable and in demonstrating why retention through Customer Relationship Management is so important.

2. Corporate customers are different from personal customers – they require different products and they have customers of their own whose needs they have to meet.

3. Understanding the real needs and not wants and then presenting the solution that meets these is critical to selling your products and services.

4. It is critical that having got a meeting – you close the sale.

Further reading

Dwight S Ritter: *Relationship Banking (Irwin)*

Ken Langdon: *Key Accounts are Different* (Pitman)

9

COLLECTING INFORMATION

Topics in this chapter

- Market research – competitor research – desk research
- Internal v. external sources
- Customer interviewing
- Analysing information

Syllabus topics covered

- Principles of customer research using internal information source.
- Data warehousing and data mining.
- Identifying cost effective external information sources.
- Effective interviews with customers.
- Analysis and evaluation of information: identifying business opportunities.

Introduction

Information is the key to making informed decisions and to being master of a brief before meeting customers. You need information to enable you to understand your customers, your own organization's capabilities, what is happening in the world, what your competitors are doing and many other things beside as well as supporting the decisions that you have to make every day. Otherwise you will be guessing or working under false assumptions.

There are many ways of obtaining information – you can use internal and external sources and of course one of the greatest sources of information about your customer is the customer himself. As the diagram overleaf shows, information is an integral part of marketing.

Figure 45: The marketing process – overview

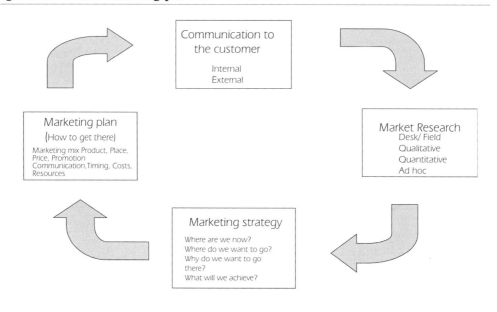

Information can come from many sources and, therefore, also in many formats. You must, therefore, put information into a consistent format and this requires a consistent framework for collating information. It is also important to understand the difference between a vast unstructured 'dump' (data) and the salient points that enable you to understand your subject (information).

Key issues for consideration are:

● For what **purpose** do I require the information (background, to support a decision, to answer a specific query etc)?

● By **when** do I need it?

● What **sort** of information do I need and in what format?

This will then enable you to collect the right amount of information in the right level of detail and also to focus your efforts on the right or optimal manner of collecting it.

9.1   Market research

This is the systematic and focused collection of information on customers, markets and competitors for subsequent analysis and usage in formulating your marketing strategy. By collecting and analysing information that is relevant it enables you to make informed and robust decisions as input into subsequent action. There are two types of research: **Desk research** and **Field research**. It is important to understand the difference between them. Desk research is usually easier and almost invariably much cheaper. It may not of course provide you with precisely what you need and you may have to resort to field research.

The objectives of research include:

- defining and evaluating your place in a market

- providing information regarding future trends in demand

- identifying customer needs and requirements

- discovering what they think of you and your offerings

- uncovering ways to delight your customers further

- providing an evaluation of advertising and promotional strategies and their content

- revealing opportunities for business development and improved competitiveness

- discovering opportunities for increasing profit/product penetration

Desk research

Before commencing any external study and commissioning field research it is always worth asking – has it been analysed before? This is usually easier and quicker and the scale of information you can access has been altered radically by the explosion of information you can obtain over the Internet. This allows you to access all (published) information globally on a subject. The surprising thing about the Internet is that so much is available – and for free! (although an unfocused search over the Internet may take a long time and result in masses of data which will take forever to analyse).

Information can come from two sources – external and internal.

Typical examples of external desk research include:

- Public library searches

- Press clippings

- Sector and published surveys

- Internet trawls

One of the major benefits of an effective and up-to-date Customer Relationship Management initiative, however, is that it should facilitate the analysis of your own customer base. This will allow you to analyse:

- Purchases made

- Comparisons with peer customers

- Patterns of consumption

- Profit from products

- Product penetration

This will provide you with unique insights because no one else will have this information. It might be necessary and desirable, however, to look externally as well – either for purposes of benchmarking, market trend analysis or competitor analysis.

Field research

This is where you have to go out and find out information first hand by talking to current and potential customers. The major types of types of field research include:

- Telephone research

- Written questionnaires

- Street interviewing

- Face-to-face interviewing

- Product tests

- Consumer panels

- Focus groups

All of these techniques have a role to play in collecting information but they result in different 'cuts' of information and some may not be appropriate. You must decide on which are the best techniques and, having obtained the information, analyse the results.

It is important that you never, ever mix up research and selling – this is called 'sugging' and it really upsets people. It can also have far-reaching and damaging effects on your relationships because people complain and will also affect the value of the exercise, making it largely unproductive.

Whenever research is undertaken, the following issues should be considered and you should have the answers clear before commissioning any research.

The Sample	Who are you going to ask? (what sort of people or segments)
The Method	How are you going to ask them?
The Questions	What are you going to ask them?
The Results	What will you do with the information?
The Cost	How much do you want to pay for the answer?
The Timescale	By when do you need the information?

These are explored in detail below and in general apply equally to personal and corporate markets.

The sample

The number of people asked is an important consideration because if you asked just one person you would get a very accurate picture of her views on anything (probably) but this would not necessarily be representative of the world at large and may lead you down a completely blind alley. How many then should you ask and what sort of people? What is a good number – is it millions, hundreds of thousands or what? Clearly there is a cost implication because the larger the number, the greater the cost increase, both in terms of carrying out the research and in analysing and interpreting the resulting data.

Fortunately a lot of research has been carried out into this area and some surprising conclusions have emerged. When you ask a number of respondents (known as the population) questions, after a certain number the percentage difference in the answer ceases to vary very much, or at least if it does then the degree of likely error can be calculated with a high degree of accuracy.

This number is known as a *'statistically significant number'* and although it needs to be calculated for each type of question, the numbers are surprisingly low. For consumer goods it is in the low hundreds and even for such emotive issues as politics it is only in low thousands. Key points are that the sample must be homogeneous, ie sharing the important characteristics – eg four-wheel car drivers in the home counties, or British owners of Portuguese villas in the Algarve – in order that the data is comparable and that conclusions are meaningful and of course targeted. This classification is known as segmentation.

The method

There are several methods of obtaining the information as mentioned above and key characteristics of each are explored below.

Telephone research

Using the telephone to collect information has one great advantage – it is cheap. One researcher can make many calls in a day without leaving an office. It is also both very focused because you are initiating the call and it is fast because interviews do not take long and the elapsed time to complete the exercise is also short.

There are some drawbacks however – often people do not like to receive unsolicited calls and it can be very difficult to use in a corporate – business to business – environment. It relies on a structured script and on obtaining answers in the same manner (eg interviewers tick boxes on a template in front of them).

Written questionnaires

This is probably the most common method of research and everyone will be familiar with it in one form or another. Unless used in the right circumstances it can be a passive method reliant on people to complete and return them and in this case inertia rules and only those with a grievance or an axe to grind return them. By combining it with other activities however, such as checking out of an hotel, installing new software or making it part of the application process for services, it can be turned into an effective method of research.

To be really effective it is best to use questionnaires that ask for boxes to be ticked or indications placed on scales. This has the advantage that it is easier and faster for the recipient to complete and also allows direct comparability of answers. It will not have perhaps the same depth as, say, a qualitative survey where respondents write comments but if it is drawn up well it is very useful and can cover more subjects than the qualitative type.

Street interviewing

This is an effective method of data collection although not always the most cost-effective because it involves people's time as researchers and may involve lots of non-value added interactions for every useful interview. Usually the researcher is situated in a busy thoroughfare and asks a few questions to eliminate candidates and ensure homogeneity (known as screening questions) before either thanking them or passing on to the next set of core questions. This is to ensure that the quote sampled is statistically significant.

It is almost exclusively used in consumer research. Segments chosen must be wide enough to be meaningful but also focused to support the conclusions you require to achieve.

Face-to-face interviewing

This is basically a structured conversation. The interviewer should have a one or two sheet guides to the questions that they want to ask. These should be ordered so as not to give too much information to the interviewee to avoid prejudicing their views.

Eg asking 'Do you like XYZ bank?' before you ask 'Of which banks are you aware?' will prejudice the answers.

You must:

- Confirm the interview beforehand with a letter or fax

- Arrive on time, and make sure the interview does not overrun

- Guide the conversation gently, but firmly

- If the interviewee is not forthcoming then make your excuses and leave

Product tests

These are widely used, especially in the consumer markets.

The manufacturer selects a group of potential buyers an offers a pre-production sample for people to use, on agreement that they report back their findings.

They are not very useful in financial services.

You should:

- Use experienced personnel (internal or external if they are not available)

- Choose an appropriate place to hold the tests (e.g. for food outside a supermarket, for audio equipment in a hall)

- Make sure that everyone who participates is given a questionnaire to complete

- Circulate during the event to get off-the-cuff remarks, and record these for later analysis

Consumer panels

Consumer panels, also called omnibus surveys, are where pre-segmented panel members fill in a diary on a regular basis.

Panel members are usually recompensed by gifts or points.

- You must:

- Use a specialist firm

Note – This is mainly for Fast Moving Consumer Goods (FMCG) only.

Focus groups

These are basically moderated group discussions.

The format is as follows:

- an audience of between 6 and 12 people with selected backgrounds is invited to the meeting. This takes place in a comfortable setting (eg like a drawing room); and may be preceeded by lunch;

- a moderator or facilitator explains the purpose of the focus group and may give some background to the topic;

- the group is then invited to discuss the relevant issues. The discussions are usually recorded (or notes are taken by an assistant);

- the moderator guides the discussion to make sure that it stays on the subject.

You must:

- ensure that the audience represents the desired segment(s);

- make sure that the audience is relaxed and feels free to speak;

- ensure that the quieter members of the group are given a chance to speak as well.

The quality of the moderator is crucial. Specialist firms are usually employed to maximize the value from the exercise.

The questions

In order to make informed decisions about anything you need the correct information. This must be based on analytical data and gives you the knowledge to make the decisions. One of the things that often emerges from research is that you actually know a lot less than you thought you did (*see* diagram).

Figure 46: Knowledge is power

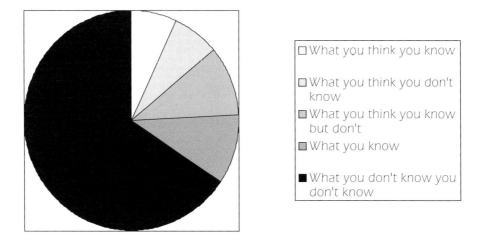

What you think you know

What you think you don't know

What you think you know but don't

What you know

What you don't know you don't know

What you know is a lot less than you think.

You must have the right level of information to make an informed decision. You must take special care, therefore, in framing the questions to ensure that you receive the correct output. The type of research chosen will also affect the type of questions. There are two types of questions:

Quantitative – based on numbers or fixed answers – eg what percentage do you pay on your mortgage, or how much are your monthly life premiums?

Qualitative – based on words – eg how do you feel that your account has been handled in the last year?

Quantitative answers are generally much easier to analyse but qualitative answers can give you more valuable insights into what people really think.

The results

What will you do with the information?

It is critical that you think this through before starting any research. What you want to do with the information should shape the nature of the questions and possibly even the manner in which it is collected. It will certainly affect the analysis and conclusions drawn and presented.

The cost

How much do you want to pay for the answer? The cost of market research can vary widely: from a few hundred pounds to many millions spent by multinationals on major consumer brands. It is relatively easy to assess the cost of market research and the procedure to follow is:

● scope out the activities that you think will be needed (eg 100 telephone calls, 20 face-to-face interviews etc) and assess the amount of time input that this requires (see below for a guide)

● identify the daily cost of either your own staff or employing people of the right calibre to do the work

● add in the preparation time for questionnaires and the time to analyse and write up the reports

A brief guide to researchers' time:

● Telephone calls – around 8 – 10 *completed* calls per working day

● Face-to-face interviews – typically only two face-to-face interviews can be accomplished a day, and if travel to other towns is required this may fall to an average of one-and-a-half – this is to allow time for the interview to be completed and written up

● Street Interviewing: around 20 – 30 a day may be accomplished, depending on the questions

● Group discussions: set aside at least a day for administration and half a day for the group. Do not forget that more than one person is required to run a group interview

● Written questionnaire: typically a response of between 1% and 3% is considered normal.

9.2   The timescale

Work backwards from when the results are required to get start date.

Produce a bar chart (sometimes called a Gantt chart) showing the various steps and the interrelationship between each of them.

Typically the stages will be as follows:

● Scope the project

● Set-up phase (eg hiring contractors, preparing questionnaires, samples, purchasing mailing lists)

● Desk research – looking to see what already exists

● Test phase (sometimes called piloting). Test a small sample of people to check your approach

● Research – there may be a number of phases, one leading to another

● Analysis – leave plenty of time for this!

● Reporting – a written report should be prepared for the benefit of others in your firm, and to provide a reference document.

Exploiting data

The amount of information you need should reflect the magnitude of the decision that you are going to make. This does not mean that you need reams of paper for an important decision – but that you do need real and pertinent information that analyses the issues and gives useful conclusions.

Figure 47: Decision-making context

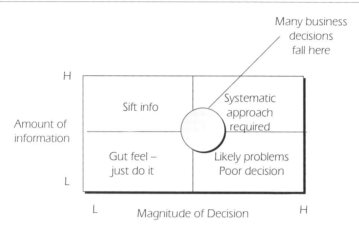

It is a balance between the **Magnitude of the decision** and the **Amount of data** you have to enable you to analyse the risks – but data should be turned into **information** that supports decisions.

There has been a true revolution in the last few decades driven by the increasing power of IT processing capability – the progressive reduction in costs both from economies of scale and from vastly increased processing capabilities – as well as the unbelievable amount of data now available publicly from the Internet. This has of course led to an equal explosion in the amount of data processed and regurgitated within organizations. Unfortunately much of the data is unusable. This is because data does not equal information – and for all too many organizations the old maxim holds true:

DRIP:

Data Rich : Information Poor.

As a result relationship managers are drowning in a sea of paper (the so-called 'paperless revolution' has in fact led to an increase in paper because people still wish to read from the paper medium and this often goes as far as then printing out e-mails writing their reply and giving them to a secretary to re-type!).

9.3   Data warehousing

What is a data warehouse?

In order to maximize usage of data – ie by turning it into information that can form the basis for decisions and conclusions – it needs to be stored and analysed. The usual method for this is to store it within a special part of the system known as a data warehouse (sometimes it can be a stand-alone system).

It has been defined as '...*the logical link between what the managers see in their decision support EIS applications and the company's operational activities...[14]*'

In other words data warehousing allows data that has already been transformed into information to enable Decision Support and Executive Information production.

A data warehouse is a Relational Database Management System (RDMS) that stores the data in such a way that it can be interrogated (slicing and dicing) for business reasons and by business users. Data warehousing makes it possible to extract operational data and overcome inconsistencies between different legacy data formats. As well as facilitating the integration of data throughout an organization regardless of location, format, or communication requirements, it is possible to incorporate additional external or even expert information.

In other words the data warehouse provides data that is already transformed and summarized which, when extracted, can form the basis for management information.

There are generally some key characteristics (after Bill Inmon[15]) ascribed to a data warehouse:

- **subject-oriented** – data is organized according to subject instead of application eg a bank using a data warehouse would organize its data by customer, DOB, location etc, instead of by different products (O/D, Loans Mortgages etc). Data organized by subject contains only the information necessary for decision-support processing.

- **integrated** – when data is kept in many separate systems or applications in an organization, encoding of data is often inconsistent. In one system gender (or sex) might be coded as 'm' and 'f'; in another by 'male' or 'female'; and in yet a third by 'man' and 'woman'; and in some (binary thinking) 0 and 1. When data is transferred into a data warehouse it is 'cleaned' so that it assumes a consistent format and coding – therefore enabling easier analysis.

- **time-variant** – a data warehouse usually contains a location for storing old data eg from 5 to 10 years ago, and in some cases even older, to be used for comparisons, trends, and forecasting. This data is not updated.

- **non-volatile** – data is not updated or changed in any way once it is in a data warehouse, but it is only loaded for subsequent access.

- **consistency** – data warehouses are designed for query processing as opposed to transaction processing, and, as a result, those databases which are linked to, or designed for, On Line Transaction Processors (OLTP) are unsuitable for data warehouses.

[14] John McIntyre: SAS Institute Inc
[15] Bill Inmon: *Building a Data Warehouse*

The structure of a data warehouse

There are five areas of a data warehouse as shown by the diagram:

- Summarized data
- Collated data
- Current data
- Older/archived data
- 'Metadata'

Figure 48: Data warehouse – structure

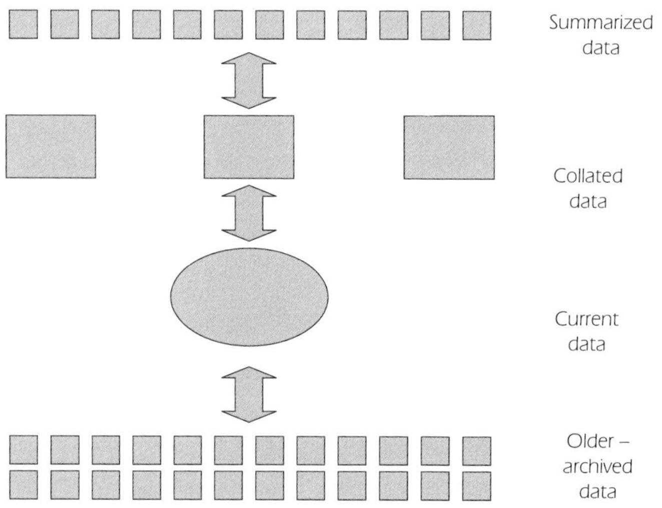

Summarized data is compact and easily accessible and can even be found outside the warehouse.

Collated or slightly summarized data is that which has been synthesised and slimmed down from lower levels of data within the warehouse. An important question when constructing a data warehouse is what period is *time-critical* as well as the characteristics of the collated data when presented.

Current data is central in importance because it:

- reflects the most recent happenings (however you have defined that), which are usually the most interesting;
- is voluminous because it is stored at the lowest level of granularity;
- needs fast access, which usually means that it is expensive and complex to manage.

Older/archived data is infrequently accessed and stored at a level of detail which is consistent with current detailed data. (It is usually stored in some form of mass storage.)

Metadata is the final component of the data warehouse and is really of a different dimension in that it is not the same as data drawn from the operational environment but is used within the system to locate the contents of the data warehouse, as a guide to the mapping of data into the warehouse and as a guide in transposing between the current data and the collated data and then the collated data and the summarized data, etc.

The following diagram shows how this might work in practice – eg for a building society. If we assume that the date is 25 June year is 2001 then the current data is 25 June 2000 to 24 June 2001. Sales data does not have to be real-time because it is unnecessary for this type of analysis and will enter the warehouse only once all processing is completed.

Details can then be summarized – sliced and diced – as you wish.

Figure 49: Data warehouse example – mortgage sales

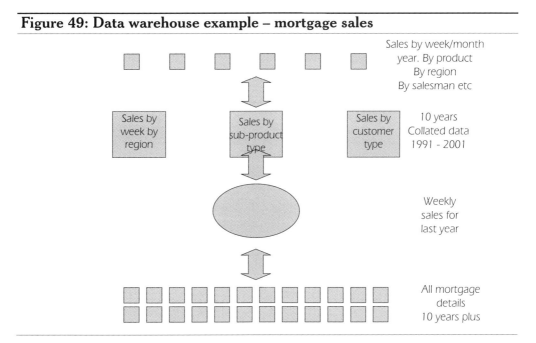

To maximize on the data warehouse you must then use a technique called data mining.

9.4   Data mining

What is data mining? The analogy comes from the mining industry and it is essentially about pulling data out and manipulating it to deliver useful information. It is also known as Knowledge Discovery in Databases.

Some definitions of Data Mining are:

> '...the nontrivial extraction of implicit, previously unknown, and potentially useful information from data. This encompasses a number of different technical approaches, such as clustering, data summarization, learning classification rules, finding dependency networks, analysing changes, and detecting anomalies.[16]'

[16] William J Frawley, Gregory Piatetsky-Shapiro and Christopher J Matheus

'...the search for relationships and global patterns that exist in large databases but are `hidden' among the vast amount of data, such as a relationship between patient data and their medical diagnosis. These relationships represent valuable knowledge about the database and the objects in the database and, if the database is a faithful mirror, of the real world registered by the database.'[17]

Data mining is about analysis of data using sophisticated software techniques to identify patterns and regularities in structured data (which is usually held in 'warehouses'). The software is responsible for finding the patterns by analysing the data and pulling out relationships and correlations. Using sophisticated analysis enables patterns to be recognized that were not previously discernable or which would take too long by normal techniques. The analogy with mining comes from the fact that you might – and indeed hope to – strike a 'lode' of lore or knowledge, which you can then exploit and use.

Data mining enables vast quantities of data to be manipulated and then analysed and as such it works upwards from the lowest pieces of data. This is further analogous to a mining operation where, frequently, a machine or miners sift large amounts of material in order to find something of value (coal, silver, diamonds etc).

Issues with data

Data mining systems rely on databases to supply the raw data for input and this raises problems in that databases tend be dynamic, incomplete, 'noisy', and large. Other problems arise as a result of the adequacy and relevance of the information stored.

Limited Information

Databases are often designed without taking data mining into account and as a result issues arise. Typically is the fact that not all data required is present. A good example for many customers is that simple data (such as date of birth) is not held as it was considered unnecessary at the time when the (typical) product was developed. For meaningful analysis of patterns of behaviour and product relevance – eg if looking at customer lifecycles – it is often critical.

'Noise'

Databases usually contain errors which contaminate the data they contain and at the same time the data has attributes which rely on subjective or measurement judgements that can cause errors which result in some items being mis-classified (for example if staff guess at gender or socio-economic class). Error in either the values of attributes or class information are known as 'noise'. Where possible this 'noise' should be eradicated or eliminated to improve the accuracy of the data. This is often known as 'data cleansing'.

Duplication

This is frequently an issue for financial services organizations where they have moved from a product-based structure to a customer-based structure and they hold several records of one

---

[17] Marcel Holshemier & Arno Siebes (1994)

customer – often containing different or conflicting data. This too needs cleaning to ensure robust and meaningful analysis.

Missing data

Missing data can be dealt with in a number of ways such as:

- ignoring missing values

- omitting the corresponding records

- inferring missing values from known values

- compute and use averages for the missing values.

Uncertainty

Uncertainty refers to the severity of the error and the degree of noise in the data. Data precision is an important consideration.

Size, updates, and irrelevant fields

Databases tend to be large and dynamic in that their contents are ever-changing as information is added, modified or removed. The problem with this from a data mining perspective is how to ensure that the rules are up-to-date and consistent with the most current information. Also the learning system has to be time-sensitive because some data values vary over time and the results and conclusions can be affected by the 'timeliness' of the data. Another issue is the relevance or irrelevance of the fields in the database – eg post codes are fundamental in many sets of analyses such as linking local market share to footfall or penetration of a branch in an area.

Uses of data mining

Data mining has the ability to assist in many areas of analysis including:

- Identifying buying patterns of customers

- Associating buying behaviour with certain 'classes of characteristics' (segments, demographics)

- Analysing responses to advertising or mailing – and therefore enabling predictive analysis of future responses and facilitating greater focus

- Fraudulent credit card use

- Fraudulent mortgage patterns (between customers, solicitors etc)

- Loyalty analysis

- Credit card spending and cross-correlation to classes of customers

- Product penetration by types and classes of customers

- Risk analysis

- Branch network product sales

9.5   Interviewing customers

One of the greatest sources of information about a customer is the customer himself. A well-planned interview can elicit much relevant information which will allow you to understand a lot about him and also to populate your database.

Interviewing

This is a key competence for a relationship manager. An interview is a structured conversation with a purpose and may take place on your premises or your client's premises and sometimes at other locations. Interviews are both effective at information gathering, for understanding issues and also relationship building. It is worth noting that a meeting with a client to discuss anything is in effect an interview.

Interview techniques

There are some very clear pointers to successful interview techniques and, because people's ability to articulate or describe their thoughts and ideas varies, it is essential to use good questioning techniques because this makes you more likely to obtain quality answers.

Ten commandments:

1.   **Establish good rapport** – this can be achieved by establishing some slight common ground of interest, recognizing their responses, and respecting opinions. This can also be shown by the tone of voice, expressions or even gestures. Good contact can be established by demonstrating attentive listening, with the interviewer showing interest, understanding, and respect for what the subjects say; by allowing them to finish what they are saying, and to proceed at their own rate of thinking and speaking – within the constraints of the timing and objectives.

2.   **Ask clear questions** – use words that make the questions easy to understand and that fit within the individual's frame of reference and that are short and jargon free.

3.   **Ask single questions** – too often there is a tendency to mix up several and, accordingly, the answer only partly meets your needs.

4.   **Use open questions** – these allow people to respond in their own terms using their own words and also to elaborate on an idea. A closed question usually elicits a yes or no response.

5.   **Ask experience-related questions before opinion questions** – as the former set the context for the latter (eg where you are dealing with a customer complaint about

staff handling 'Describe the events that took place' followed by 'How do you feel about it?') and gets facts before emotion.

6. **Place the questions in sequence** – this refers to using a special kind of questioning technique called 'funnelling', which means asking from general to specific, from broad to narrow.

7. **Probe and follow up questions** – to broaden the response to a question, to increase the depth of the data being obtained, and to give clues to the interviewee about the level of response that is desired. This can be done through a direct link to an answer – 'Could you elaborate on that point?' or 'Do you have further examples of this?' Note that sometimes non-verbal signs can encourage the interviewee to go on – a mere nod or just a pause. Repeating significant words from the answer can also lead to further elaboration – eg 'exporting to Indonesia?' or '…so you switched to invoicing in euros?'

8. **Avoid questions that might be sensitive** – it is advisable to avoid deep questions which may irritate the informants, possibly resulting in an interruption of the interview or a closing down.

9. **Keep control** but encourage wide-ranging answers – sometimes you have to let the interviewees 'travel' wherever they like, but a rough checklist of ideas or areas the former want to explore is useful – experienced interviewers should always be in control of the conversation which they guide and re-orient as necessary.

10. **Interpret the answers** – throughout the interview you must clarify and extend the meanings of their answers to avoid misinterpretations on their part. This is often achieved by repeating and summarizing what has been said – eg 'So you did that and then that?' or 'So you need working capital finance of £5 million to cover exports to Afghanistan?' This allows them to confirm your understanding, or to clarify your misinterpretation.

Key steps in preparing for an interview

Before the interview

- be clear as to the purpose and objectives of your interview
- carry out all relevant research:
  - customer history
  - products
  - economic analysis
  - current restrictions on customers etc
- if you are the one who prepares the setting for the interview make sure that the venue and time is satisfactory. Ensure that you remove any physical or psychological barriers and

that you have privacy – discussing overdraft requirements or discussing unauthorized borrowings in an open office or a public area is not conducive to effective interviewing!

- if you are visiting a client for an interview make sure you have communicated effectively with your client about the point of the meeting and the timing and duration. Diarize it! (NB as a general rule you should only have **one** diary!)

- dress fittingly for the interview but be comfortable

- ensure you have prepared for the interview ie you clearly understand the purpose of the interview; you have researched the background needed for the interview; and you have an interview plan and prepared questions/offers etc.

Commencing the interview

- be on time if you are travelling – if you are meeting the customer at your premises then also be on time!

- introduce yourself and your role properly. Make the customer feel welcome – despite the nature of the interview. Shake hands and smile and pass the time of day with small talk. Establish rapport quickly and easily – be warm and natural

- Offer a drink, perhaps

- re-confirm the objectives and structure of the interview as well as the timings – confirm that that is the client's understanding too and that they do have the time required

- establish any rules of 'confidentiality' if these are clearly important

- take notes and explain that you will send written confirmation afterwards where appropriate

The main body

- move into the main part of the interview clearly and professionally. Keep your objectives in mind and work to your plan

- introduce the main topic early to ensure that you achieve your objectives

- use an effective questioning technique – with well-structured open-ended questions (see above)

- when you have opened up an area of questioning then use shorter probing questions to penetrate the area. Stay with the topic until you have the information you want. Be sensitive, however, to your client's feelings. Do not over-pressurize them

- avoid closed questions which prompt a Yes/No answer – or use them to good effect! '... so what you mean is that you need a loan of £100,000 for 6 months?' – either a yes or no clarifies the position

- do not use leading questions or the answer you receive may not be accurate or complete

- summarize periodically to confirm understanding and to keep to your plan

- (try to) control the pace of the interview!

- observe and use silences or pauses intelligently. Some people need longer to answer and collect their thoughts than others – give them that time. Listen by active listening ie good body posture, eye contact and logical progression of answers and next questions

- keep the rapport going – smile, offer tea etc

- be sensitive and flexible. If your original interview plan is clearly off track – then clarify the area for discussion. If you lose the thread do not waffle, acknowledge it, move onto another topic and ask if you may return to the original line later

- invite questions and answer them or agree to find out the information

Closing

- finish on a high note wherever possible

- summarize and explain the next steps

- close the interview nicely

- arrange the date of next meeting and/or lines of communication if you need to follow up

- thank your client

- shake hands and depart or conduct them off the premises

Interview reports

Straight after the interview write up your interview notes while the meeting is still fresh in your mind – it is amazing how points fade rapidly. Do whatever you said that you would do – eg write at once to confirm key points. Put in hand research or proposals for permission.

Common faults with interview technique

- lateness because of poor planning or incompetence

- letting initial impressions colour your thoughts – HALO or HORNS effect

- interviewer talking too much and allowing insufficient 'airtime' for the interviewee

- allowing the interviewee to take control of the interview

- waffle or rambling sentences that lead nowhere – from either side

- unspecified, confused objectives

- bias and prejudice – the influence of your dislikes or stereotyping

- unsystematic/poor planning eg having too many questions for the time available

- failure to establish rapport

Key learning points

1. Information about your customers is vital not only to understanding their needs and wants but also to formulating solutions that address them.

2. Data warehouses provide an excellent mechanism for collating and aggregating data.

3. The data needs 'cleaning' to be of real use.

4. Data mining allows you to interrogate the data warehouse and undertake trend analysis.

5. You must be well prepared for interviews/meetings and run them properly. Be clear as to your objectives and meet them.

6. Write up interviews/meetings as soon as you have finished – while they are still fresh in your mind.

Further reading

Baden Eunson: *Communicating with Customers*

10

BUILDING RELATIONSHIPS

Topics in this chapter
- Understanding and managing customer expectations
- Developing customer confidence
- Cost-effective value adding
- Planning and delivering propositions to customers
- Managing face-to-face customer contacts
- Managing remote contacts
- Managing multi-contacts

Syllabus topics covered
- Retail and business customer profiling.
- Relationship life cycles.
- Understanding and managing customer expectations.
- Building relationships by adding value to customers cost effectively.

Introduction

Establishing a relationship with a customer takes time and develops over the lifetime of the relationship. It is a function of the number of transactions, the quality of service received and costs associated with it. Good management can improve both the rate of relationship development and the likelihood of customer retention.

The challenge for any organization is to ensure that its efforts are focused on those customers who deliver the revenue and profitability that it desires. Relationship management is costly and therefore is not to be wasted on customers who lose you money.

10.1   Cost-effective value adding

The link between revenue is often assumed but it is not usually true that those generating revenue generate profit. First Union in the USA undertook an analysis of its customer base by splitting its customers into ten segments for profitability. It received a shock when it found that those in the bottom segment generated most revenue thereby demonstrating an inverse correlation between revenue and profit[18]. This means that staff are recruiting customers that destroy value to the bank!

In the following simple diagram different customer segments have been plotted to show whether they are generating value or destroying value for the organization. Of the six segments

● two generate the value

● two consume as much capital as they generate and

● two actually destroy value!

Figure 50:   Managers should identify the contribution customer segments make to value

---

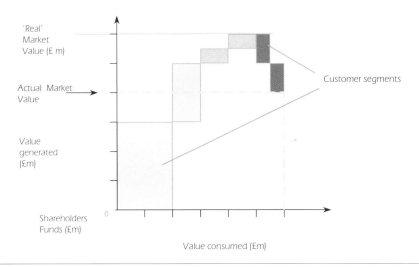

From this (simple example) analysis the organization needs to manage out the poorly performing segments and try to improve the medium segments by increasing charges, or reducing costs. Business often calls for tough decisions and this is a case where the need for these is amply demonstrated.

Pareto's law holds true with frightening accuracy in banking. Several recent studies showed the following[19]:

● For one bank 15% of its customers were responsible for 85% of profit

[18] Jerry Cover: 'Profitability Analysis – a necessary tool for success in the 21st century' (*ABA Banking Journal* 1999)
[19] ibid

- In small business banking less than 10% of the clients generated 90% of profit

- For a typical portfolio of retail customers 20% of accounts generated 200% of the overall return and up to 50% of accounts generated losses (destroyed value to the bank)

It is critical, therefore, that relationship management focuses on that top 20% of 'Pareto' customers. Clearly the major prize for an organization is to manage out the unprofitable ones and move marginal customers farther up the profitability ladder.

This needs to be handled carefully – see the difficulties encountered by Halifax when trying to discourage cash-heavy clients (February 2002).

10.2   Understanding and managing customer expectations

There are several types of customers and they will all have different needs. These include:

- new

- renewing

- spasmodic

- inactive

and within these categories they may be:

- low value

- low volume

- high value

- high volume

and some will be

- lapsed/inert

It is clear that in general you want high-value customers – but of course in the broad sweep of things your customers will be a mix. The critical element is ensuring that your accounts receive the level of service that their value to the organization merits.

This means that low-value accounts do not receive high levels of personal service – or if they do then they will pay for them. In fact you should give low level of service (but not quality) for low-value clients and also manage some of those out. For inert or inactive clients you can just write them off after a while – and if they re-activate, re-animate the account.

The diagram overleaf shows how different customer segments have different priorities with the same product – depending on their needs. Some value tax minimization highly while others are looking for good value. Meeting these needs is a major challenge but one that is made easier when the underlying needs are understood,

Figure 51: Differing priorities by segment

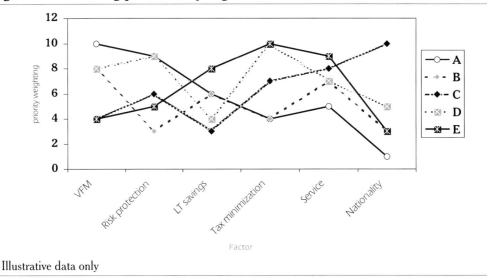

Illustrative data only

When meeting customers it is important to manage their expectations. This involves understanding their needs and expectations and then making it perfectly clear to them what they will receive as a customer. This means that prior to the meeting – or if it is an exploratory meeting immediately thereafter – you need to develop an account plan. Depending on the type of customer, this may be a detailed document or merely a few general jottings to serve as a framework for informing them.

When meeting with customers – remember that you are both negotiating. The customer is under no obligation to take your offering and similarly you are under no obligation to supply him. The best solution is a win-win where both parties feel that they have got at least part of what they want. The diagram below shows the possible results from a meeting.

Figure 52: Negotiation

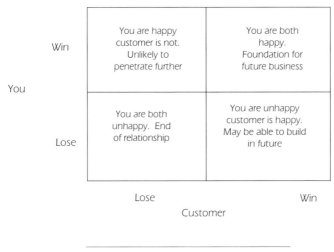

If you are unable to achieve a win-win the next best is customer wins – as long as it is not too bad for you. This at least allows you to have another crack at his business and change the terms to be more favourable next time.

Part of achieving the win-win is by managing expectations so that what you can do for your customer becomes the 'expected' and therefore fits.

10.3   New customers

There are some key objectives that you must have when meeting new customers:

Gain understanding

- Introduce your organization and its total capabilities to them – even if they are not all relevant at this stage – you do not yet know his likely future needs
- Assess the potential short-term revenue
- Assess the longer-term revenue opportunities
- Review possible offerings that may be useful to him
- Ascertain what the competition is and what they are offering
- For a corporate
  - Understand the structure
  - Establish who the decision-makers are
  - Learn the decision-making process
  - Understand the buying cycles
  - View premises (if the first visit does not take place there)
- Arrange a follow-up meeting

Understand requirements

- Respond to a particular request
- Identify issues
- Offer a service or a series of services
- Further build on the relationships

Presenting a proposal

- Prepare the proposal – core/basic
- Prepare variations

- Identify negotiation points

- Present the proposal

- Check focus of the proposal

- Obtain feedback/reactions

- Negotiate the terms

- If necessary fix the next meeting

Doing the deal

- Obtain the purchase

- Sign the contract

- If necessary introduce other personnel

- Further build the relationship

- Sort out any immediate issues

- Look for other opportunities

- Establish start dates

- Agree next steps

- Fix next meeting

Orphans

These are customers who have nobody looking after them. This is usually because there has been a change in personnel. They are often a very good source of business as picking them up and managing them can pay dividends. Depending on the time since they were properly managed this can sometime be difficult and the life-time value needs to be considered to judge whether these types are worth the effort.

Diaries

These are critical aids in relationship management. Time is money in the old saying and this was never more true than for a relationship manager. To maximize the benefits from dealing with clients it is important that time is prioritized. This means planning well in advance. The things to plan include:

- Recurrent items that always take place – such as annual or semi-annual reviews.

- Visits – to be correlated to other activities to maximize time lost in travelling

- Internal reviews of profitability

● Board/executive presentations

● Telephone calls/meetings

You cannot manage the past – it has happened so you need to be continually looking forward.

With electronic diaries now available to virtually everyone it is possible to run a real-time diary that others in the organization can have access to as well so they can see when you are free and use it to ask for meetings etc.

Effective usage of diaries is an important element in managing client relationships. By continually demonstrating that you are on top of his needs you cement the relationship further.

The Customer Relationship Management database should also be used for generating automatic diary reminders and linked into personal diaries to ensure nothing key is missed (loan anniversaries or maturities, important events – children attaining majority etc.) so that meetings can be planned in a timely fashion.

Sales funnels

Using a sales funnel is a very useful way of managing sales pipelines because it serves as a diagrammatic way of showing where you are with your proposals. You can use it to focus your attention on those that are closest to completion and also to demonstrate progress to superiors. It will also highlight where extra help is needed in good time so you can manage the lead through. By using reasonable discount factors for the different levels of proposals you can put a 'discounted' or realistic value on your work and demonstrate that you are adding value.

Taking a simplistic example where a relationship manager has three levels of business – suspects, prospects and proposals. He or she could place discount factors on them of say 25%, 55% and 75% to give values of business –

No.	Type	Value	Discount	Expected value
		£	%	£
45	suspects	2.8m	25%	0.7m
30	prospects	1.8m	55%	0.9m
18	proposals	1.2m	75%	0.9m
93		**5.8m**	**43%**	**2.5m**

This also enables everyone to see the value of the levels and what proportion are taken forward to close.

Figure 53: New sales model

3D Sales funnel

Outer ring = identified
Inner ring = qualified
Centre = close

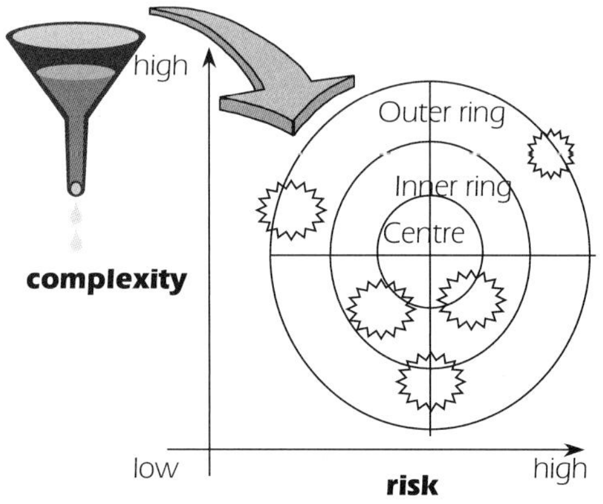

- Place opportunities on funnel with size representing size of opportunity
- Quadrant equals risk/complexity of opportunity to bank
- Gradually guide the opportunity down the funnel
- Minimize the risk where possible
- Use funnel to 'self-coach'

The information from the sales funnel can then be translated into a report – eg:

Stage in Sales	Deals	Revenue	Need Management input	Need specialist Input
Outer	24	N/A	7	6
Inner	12	£7.0M	4	5
Centre	6	£5.4M	2	1

This allows management to see likely trends, to map progress and to take action to support sales staff. By plotting the business on the sales funnel in terms of risk and complexity it further allows a detailed analysis of ancillary issues to assist in closing them.

Key learning points

1. It is not always true that those generating revenue generate profit.

2. Relationship management is costly and, therefore, is not to be wasted on customers who lose you money.

3. Part of achieving the win-win is by managing expectations so that what you can do for your customer becomes the 'expected' and, therefore, fits.

4. It is important to manage sales leads intensively to ensure that you reap the benefit of your efforts.

Further reading

Stone and Woodcock: *Relationship Marketing*

Mark Stewart: *Keep the Right Customer*

Ned Herman: *The Whole Business Brain*

11

CUSTOMER RELATIONSHIP MANAGEMENT AND IT

Topics in this chapter

- Where IT fits in – its proper role
- Types of IT support (OLAP/OLTP)
- Ensuring effectiveness
- Choosing a system

Syllabus topics covered

- Data warehousing and data mining.
- Planning and managing Customer Relationship Management projects.
- Target setting.

Introduction

Information Technology (IT) is seen by many (especially within the IT industry) as a strategic enabler that allows a wonderful life when used. For users it is often seen as a barrier to their being able to do anything of use – while at the same time being peppered with useless reports, fiendishly complex processes and a lack of support. The answer of course lies somewhere in between.

This book is not a treatise on IT but it is helpful for staff to understand where IT fits in with their day-to-day business and so outlines only are given here.

For a Customer Relationship Management system great care is needed to make sure that the system will deliver what you want and it is not just a system that the vendor says can support your Customer Relationship Management needs. In principal Customer Relationship Management technologies should support two distinct areas:

- back office customer data aggregation and analysis

- front office end-user data presentation and manipulation.

Customer Relationship Management solutions are built on relational databases, often called 'middleware' because it sits between the main (sometimes called legacy) systems that handle the transaction processing and the user interfacing systems that deliver the data. Between the processing area (back office) and the users (front office) there are usually many different technologies that facilitate analysis and presentation. The end-user may be a member of staff or the customer.

End-user interfaces can be in the banking hall, at a member of staff's workstation, in a call centre, or even at a remote location such as at an ATM machine, on the telephone, or via the Internet. This last point is very useful as because of the boon in Internet usage a by-product of Internet banking and total delivery channel solutions is the Customer Relationship Management technology on which they have been based.

Internet banking products were frequently constructed around relational database technology that collects data together and then facilitates slicing and dicing of customer information online. As a result some IT companies that supported the Internet rush are now claiming to offer Customer Relationship Management technology – based around their Internet developments.

11.1 What should a Customer Relationship Management system contain?

A good Customer Relationship Management system utilizes many tools to enable the following processes:

- Aggregating vast quantities of customer data into a single repository;
- Cost accounting analysis;
- Profitability analysis;
- Marketing campaign building;
- Sales tracking;
- Incentive compensation;
- Customer delivery.

Each of these processes may require a number of programs or technologies to provide a solution. Putting together a Customer Relationship Management system is difficult, because it does not usually come off the shelf as a 'plug 'n' play' application. It requires a consistent technology platform that is scalable and supportable across all delivery channels. This means that careful planning is required and it is not possible to produce a Customer Relationship Management solution overnight.

Developing a Customer Relationship Management system

For some organizations it will be necessary to develop a new Customer Relationship Management system. This does not mean replacing your legacy systems (or not necessarily, depending on circumstances) but does mean being very clear as to what you need and what you expect it to deliver in terms of support. This might be supplied internally or you may need to commission external suppliers to deliver all or part of what may be required.

Figure 54: Generic Systems Design Steps

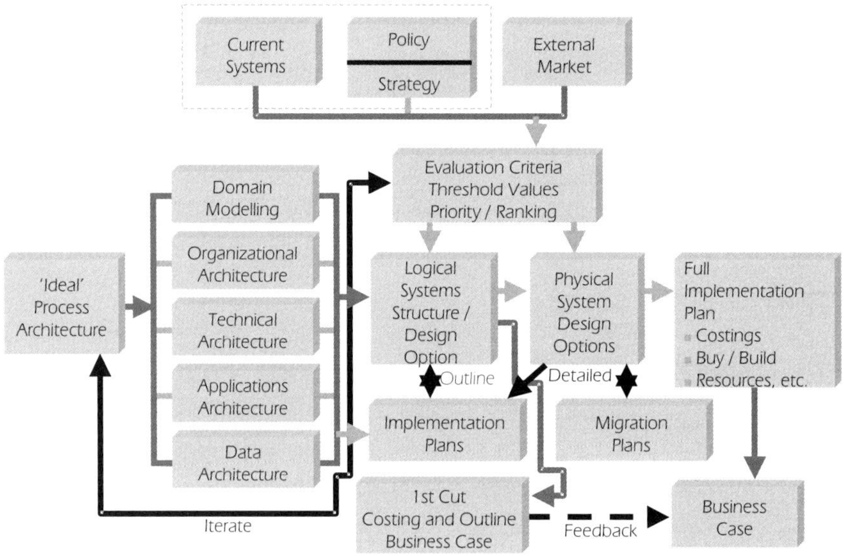

The diagram above shows the steps necessary to arrive at a new system – based on user input from processes etc. This also shows how complex it can be!

Systems design

The business objectives of Customer Relationship Management must be clearly articulated before any decisions are made and given that the next steps are to develop the systems design. The key issues here are to agree on:

● **Outputs** – what will be produced and who will need access to the outputs? What form will they be in and what will be the volumes, frequency and types of outputs?

● **Inputs** – these will be greatly influenced by the outputs – for example whether it needs to be on-line access for outputs would determine that you will need on-line input. Key considerations would include:

  ● Data collection methods

- Sources of data (internal/external)

- Volumes

- Design of input layouts etc

- **Files** – inputs are processed against the files to produce necessary output; key considerations here include:

  - Storage and media

  - Methods of file organization and access

  - File security

  - Record layouts

- **Procedures** – how the system runs and how manual interfaces work

The design sequence – criteria

There are some key criteria that will shape the design:

- Purpose – what it is for – as defined in the business case

- Cost/benefit – will it deliver what is required at an acceptable cost and on time?

- Workflows – these should be optimized

- Specialization v. simplification v. standardization – what degree will be required and what is desirable?

- Modularity of system – can it be expanded later on if that is desired?

- Reliability of hardware and software – and of the external third-party supplier if that is the case

- Data form – both for collection and for presentation back to users

- Interfaces with existing systems

- Audit trails

- Time criticality – processing times – offline versus online, volumes of usage and modes of access

Systems specification

The next step is to draw up a systems specification that is the documentation of the system and will help as a record of what was intended, as a blueprint for development and as a communication tool. This is the first step in documentation of systems which is crucial as the organization moves forward. It should contain:

- Summary

- Objectives of the system and why this design has been chosen

- Systems description

- Detailed specification of:

  - Input files

  - Output files

  - Master files

  - Source documents

  - Output documents

- Programme specification – specifically

  - Flowcharts of each programme

  - Test data and expected results

  - Stop/start, file checking, error-checking procedures

  - Controls

  - Relationship between procedures and systems

- Implementation procedures

  - Detailed timetable

  - Conversion procedures

  - Change-over procedures as appropriate including systems testing

- Equipment required and maintenance

- User instructions

- Sign off and acceptance-testing details

Once the system specification has been drawn up and agreed the next step is to develop the software etc. This might be carried out in-house or the decision may have been made to use external suppliers. If that is the case then it will be necessary to ask for tenders and run a selection process.

Project management of a Customer Relationship Management initiative

A frequent question is: How does a Customer Relationship Management project differ from other projects, for example, from ERP programs? The answer is that the techniques used are similar, but a Customer Relationship Management project has a different emphasis. Many of the projects within organizations that people have experienced have been IT driven and as a result they have a jaundiced view (often quite rightly) of what is involved.

A Customer Relationship Management project, on the other hand, is focused much more on the customer and his or her interfaces with your staff. As a result, therefore, it needs much greater involvement from business people across the organization. As business people frequently lack the skills and experience of project and programme management, these skills must be obtained early in the process. Where an organization has an in-house consultancy they will probably have adequate understanding of the skills required. If they do not bring these skills or obtain them from outside, the programme teams will experience cultural and communication problems. IT and business people need to understand each other and work together more closely to create the innovative technology-supported ideas that will result in a successful Customer Relationship Management programme and yield sustainable competitive advantage and enhanced shareholder value.

Another big difference is that Customer Relationship Management is closely enmeshed with successful changing of behaviours, attitudes and relationships in general, so cultural change management plays a far greater part. This fact also means that Customer Relationship Management needs a far greater degree of involvement and leadership from senior executives to drive and enforce the changes and create the right environment.

The structure of the work in Customer Relationship Management projects is also slightly different. Work on communication and buy-in is more protracted, and there is a far greater need for planning and prioritization because of the wider scope. Also, deliverables need to be seen quicker and faster in Customer Relationship Management to build up momentum and support. Finally, the benefit focus is different; Customer Relationship Management has many more 'soft' and longer-term benefits.

Using data

Customer Relationship Management requires data for analysis and process and, therefore, needs both OLAP and OLTP support (see below).

Comparison of OLAP and OLTP

OLAP is short for On-Line Analytical Processing and focuses on the analysis of data to provide information (typically EIS/MIS). This data is analysed from databases and then transposed, usually into pre-set formats, either to produce reports or to allow staff to access and produce their own reports for management purposes. The database itself is organized so that related data can be rapidly retrieved across multiple dimensions.

OLTP is short for On-line Transaction Processing in which the system retrieves and updates a small number of records. For example with a typical customer order entry for a change of address the OLTP transaction might retrieve all of the data relating to a specific customer and then insert a new address in the appropriate fields for the customer. Information would be selected from fields concerning the customer, customer number and detail lines. The relationships between the records are simple and only a few records are actually retrieved or updated by a single transaction.

These two types of processing are usually contained on different servers.

OLAP

OLAP database servers support common analytical operations including: consolidation, drill-down, and 'slicing and dicing'.

- Consolidation – involves the aggregation of data such as simple roll-ups or complex expressions involving interrelated data. For example, sales offices can be rolled-up to districts and districts rolled-up to regions

- Drill-Down – OLAP data servers can also go in the reverse direction and automatically display detail data which comprises consolidated data. This is called drill-down. Consolidation and drill-down are inherent properties of OLAP servers

- Slicing and Dicing – this refers to the ability to look at the database from different viewpoints. One slice of the sales database might show all sales of product type within regions. Another slice might show all sales by sales channel within each product type. Slicing and dicing is often performed along a time axis in order to analyse trends and find patterns.

OLAP queries are typically transactions which, on-line:

- Need to access very large amounts of data, eg several days/weeks of account movements

- Analyse the relationships between the elements – withdrawals, deposits, cheques, DDs, standing orders etc

- Involve aggregating data

- Compare that data over (hierarchical) time periods – daily, weekly monthly, quarterly, yearly

- Present data in different perspectives eg values by customer by branch by product by channels by location

- Involve complex analysis – eg lifetime value of a set of customers by branch and variances to the norm

- (in theory) offers fast response so that analysis can take place in order to provide timely information that will enable decisions to be taken that are time-critical and relevant

OLAP servers can hold complex and multidimensional data in a compressed form. This is accomplished by using special storage arrangements and compression techniques that maximize space utilization. 'Dense' data (where there is data in existence for a high percentage of components cells) is stored separately from 'sparse' data (where a significant percentage of cells are empty). By optimizing space utilization, OLAP servers can minimize data storage needs, thus making it possible to analyse exceptionally large amounts of data within the server. (Anyone who has used 'defrag' in Windows on a PC will have seen this type of compression and optimization in process.)

OLTP

A database that has been constructed to support OLTP will be unsuitable to support OLAP. This is because the requirements are different. OLTP has different objectives such as maximising transaction capacity and typically having hundreds of tables in order not to lock out users etc. OLAP needs to support queries.

OLTP systems are used to process data continually. When the data has been processed it is then placed back in the repository – from whence it can be analysed. It is, therefore, impossible for it to be used to pull off queries because the data is inconsistent and changing, duplicate entries exist, entries can be missing and there is no historical data within it, which is necessary to support trend analysis.

The OLTP data must be kept separate from any OLAP data and indeed it is usual for the OLAP data to be sourced from several places.

Data in an OLTP must, therefore, be transferred into the OLAP database to facilitate the analysis. It must first of all be 'cleansed'.

Cleaning data

Data cleansing is an important aspect of creating an efficient data warehouse in that it is the removal of certain aspects of operational data, such as low-level transaction information, which slows down the query times. The cleansing stage has to be as dynamic as possible to accommodate all types of queries – even those which may require low-level information. Data should be extracted from production sources at regular intervals and pooled centrally but the cleansing process has to remove duplication and reconcile differences between various styles of data collection.

Key learning points

1. In principle Customer Relationship Management technologies should support two distinct areas:

    back office customer data aggregation and analysis

    front office end-user data presentation and manipulation.

2. Customer Relationship Management solutions are built on relational databases, often called 'middleware' because it sits between the main (sometimes called legacy) systems that handle the transaction processing and the user interfacing systems that deliver the data. It needs to support a number of users in many different locations and channels.

3. It is critical that a Customer Relationship Management programme be sponsored and run by the business and not IT.

Further reading

FT: *Mastering Strategy*

12

DEVELOPING A STRATEGY

Topics in this chapter

- Setting objectives
- Understanding capabilities

Syllabus topics covered

- The importance of effective Customer Relationship Management strategies as an integral part of effective financial services marketing strategies for retail and business customers.
- Customer Relationship Management as part of a customer service quality strategy.
- The business environment of Customer Relationship Management: legal, ethical, economic, competitive and social.
- Customer Relationship Management in other business sectors eg retailing (home shopping, loyalty cards, globalization, distribution management).
- The role of Customer Relationship Management in business strategy.
- Understanding service quality.
- Target setting.
- Measuring performance of Customer Relationship Management.

Introduction

Before embarking on a Customer Relationship Management initiative it is fundamental that the strategy is thought through. This is so that it will be planned and executed well but also such that it supports the organization's objectives and really delivers value to the organization and the customer.

12.1   Key questions

There are a number of questions that must be addressed in setting up a Customer Relationship Management initiative:

Why are we undertaking a Customer Relationship Management initiative?

The answer might seem intuitive but it must nevertheless be clearly articulated and based on well thought through issues, analysis facts with clear goals and benefits. It is important so that there is no misunderstanding later on as to what it was intended to achieve and also to gain executive buy-in and commitment to the overall ideas. It is important to understand the cost benefit argument to 'prove' the worth.

Customer Relationship Management adds value only where it supports overall strategic goals – such as those expressed in shareholder value. The prime financial objective of a firm is to maximize the wealth of its shareholders but this does not mean excluding the needs of all other stakeholders. Value creation requires:

- excellent service to customers

- well-motivated employees with the right skills and customer-facing ethos

- 'premium' cash flow – cash earned over and above the 'cost of equity capital'

- managers acting like owners

The rewards can be substantial and companies that have benefited from adopting SHV include: Barclays, Coke, Lloyds TSB, Siemens, Merck, GE, Nordstrom, Dow, Disney, Prudential, NU, Boots. Customer Relationship Management is an important pillar of this concept.

Are we structured correctly to deliver Customer Relationship Management?

This involves thinking about how you should be structured, what is the gap between the desired state and the present position and what action needs to be taken to close it. Structure, in this context, means such items as:

- authority levels – and ensuring that they are 'close to the customer'. This does not mean physically – or not necessarily so; eg delegated authority to a call centre is close to the customer in terms of being able to give decisions to customers during an interaction

- information flows – and whether they are sufficient and of adequate timeliness to support the Customer Relationship Management. Also whether they are accurate and detailed enough

- responsibility – for managing customers or groups of customers across often widely diversified constituent parts of an organization

- channels – do we have the right ones – the right number – and are they sufficiently integrated in information flow terms to enable us to gather the data and offer a seamless Customer Relationship Management service across them?

How will you manage the delivery of Customer Relationship Management?

This is about how the Customer Relationship Management programme is effected and what is required to make it work in practice on a day-to-day basis. Do you have:

- well thought through policies that cover interrelationships between parts of the group, different groups of customers and the levels of service that they will receive?

- procedures that will explain and govern how staff will operate under Customer Relationship Management?

- systems that support the information gathering and synthesis, analysis and reporting – and will staff have the required access to them?

- people – what skills, knowledge and attributes will they require. How they will be rewarded and what training will they need? – it is easy to change the first three but making people change and change effectively is much more difficult. Many changes have foundered on the rocks of people resistance.

12.2   Strategic breadth and depth

In setting a Customer Relationship Management strategy it must not only link with corporate and competitive strategies but percolate through the whole organization from the top – organizational structure down to customers.

There are a number of key steps that must be followed in setting the strategy:

1. Define the segments

2. Understand the customer needs

3. Define the objectives

4. Define policies – ie the different 'qualifications' for different levels of service

5. Formulate the approach

6. Develop the offerings

7. Make offers

8. Obtain feed back and feedback through 4

The following diagram shows how Customer Relationship Management percolates down from the top, through competitive strategies, channels, individual outlets and down to customers.

Figure 55: CRM Strategy

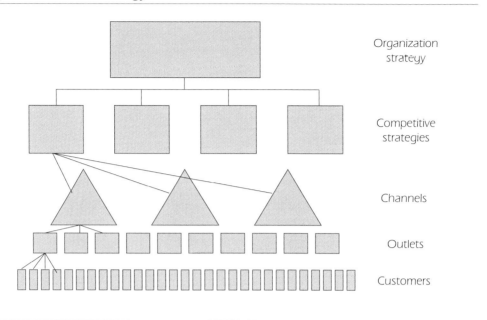

Organization strategy

Competitive strategies

Channels

Outlets

Customers

Channels

A recent survey by *Consultants Advisory* magazine[20] of clients' usage of different channels gave a very wide spread use of multi-channels, underlining the difficulties in managing relationships. 12% of respondents were in financial services and the same survey found that while respondents expected the usage of other channels to grow significantly in the future, **they did not expect a fall in other types of channels**.

Accordingly the strategy must be cognisant of multi-channel contacts and be able to handle these. This principally means that data must be scrupulously recorded by staff, so that the database is up to date and that all organizational touch points have access to the same data. Thus they will be able to offer a seamless service to the customer.

Given that customers can now access organizations through many channels relatively easily – their expectations are now that they will receive the same level of service across them all. This means that your customer-facing processes must be the same across all aspects of the organization – in as far as managing the customers is concerned and that the staff must all receive the same levels of training.

What this means is that your Customer Relationship Management must support access by customers through any and all channels that exist within your organization. You cannot just develop Customer Relationship Management for one channel only. It will not work for your customers who have the right to and will demand the same levels of service across the whole of your organization.

[20] See p 75 ([10]).

Figure 56: Channel usage

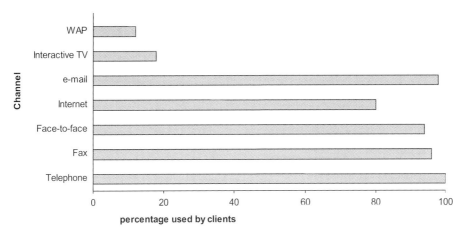

percentage used by clients

Source: Consultants Advisory/PMP

Once there is an understanding of the vision for Customer Relationship Management and buy-in to the work has been obtained, then a Customer Relationship Management strategy can be written, together with a project business case and high-level framework. An important input into this work is an assessment of the Customer Relationship Management capabilities needed to support the Customer Relationship Management strategy and the current state of those capabilities. With this information in hand, all the project initiatives can be identified, planned with the relevant governance and prioritized with overall Customer Relationship Management build and benefits in mind.

12.2 Value – objectives of a Customer Relationship Management

The model (Figure 57) as developed and used by Rank Xerox demonstrates the linkages between key sets of stakeholders in generating value – employees, customers and shareholders.

It exemplifies that it is important to consider all stakeholders (although not necessarily in the same proportion) when formulating strategies. In implementing a Customer Relationship Management programme it is vital that all these parts be recognized and that they are included in the thinking and strategic implementation.

Once the business case and high-level framework are agreed on, the programme team can get down to detailed planning. Many organizations pay insufficient attention to this phase, and yet, in hindsight, when they review success (or not) realize (and wish) that if they had spent longer on it; it would have saved wasted effort, delays, frustration, false starts and an uncoordinated approach and fragmented outputs.

Figure 57: Value-added model

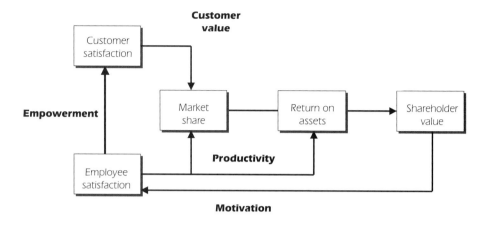

A key feature of the planning and design stage is the detailed phasing and prioritizing of all the Customer Relationship Management initiatives identified, together with estimates of risk and dependencies. It is in this phase that detailed analysis is carried out and used to support assertions of benefits, costs and the Customer Relationship Management metrics to be used.

It is very important that prioritizing items is carried out in conjunction with all the project teams in order to get buy-in and ownership. To do this well, some people set up model or pilot offices to create and test new ways of working.

Audits of data, process and technology can be done in this phase to give insight into the detail of what needs to be done when. It is following this phase that real system implementation can begin.

The environment in which financial services organizations operate is changing, technology is changing and delivering new opportunities on a massively different scale than hitherto and of course customer expectations are changing. As a result, therefore, it is often difficult for organizations to be sure of what they need to do to develop customer relationships, or what is possible in the 'brave new world' Customer Relationship Management model of working.

Taking a step-by-step approach to Customer Relationship Management gives organizations the opportunity to test and pilot new ways of working in an incubation unit, before they are introduced into the mainstream operations. This breaks process re-engineering down into less risky and more manageable chunks. The benefits are that:

- The results can be fed into the evolving strategy

- Control is greater and contained

- Mistakes can be made and learnt from in a less risky environment

- The program can monitor the implementation and ensure benefits are likely to be delivered

- Staff feel they are helping to build the new organization, so there is greater buy-in

- Pilot staff can be used to coach during full implementation

- Customers can have their inputs

The capabilities of technology can be explored and pushed to new limits.

Focusing your strategic effort

Analysis[21] shows that there is an inverse relationship between where marketing investment is made and those customers that deliver value (see diagram below). Changing this relationship is critical to improving both retention and also to increasing lifetime value. This analysis supports the assertion that market penetration (in terms of customers' wallet share) is the way ahead for organizations.

Figure 58: The Investment/Profit paradox

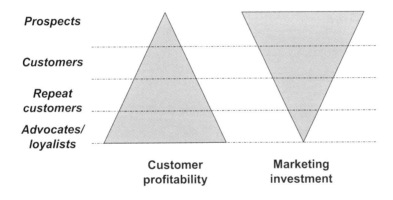

Given that the lifetime value from customers increases disproportionately with the time they spend with you it is better to focus your marketing effort on the excellent (in terms of revenue generation) customer segments that you already have and less on new customers.

This is known as 'farming' ie developing the customer base that you have, rather than going out and trying to gain new ones, often *at the expense of existing customers*. This is known as 'hunting' and is generally less productive than the former approach.

---

[21] Abram, Hawker plc: *Customer Value Management* (web paper 1998)

Key learning points

1. In setting a Customer Relationship Management strategy it must not only link with corporate and competitive strategies but percolate through the whole organization from the top – organizational structure down to customers.

2. Customer Relationship Management means that you must deliver the same quality of service to customers across all channels – whether it be face-to-face, via telephone or over the Internet.

3. Existing profitable – or potentially profitable – customers are, by and large, more fertile ground for exploitation of products than seeking new ones; and the return on investment is usually much better.

4. Given that the lifetime value from customers increases disproportionately with the time they spend with you it is better to focus your marketing effort on the excellent (in terms of revenue generation) customer segments that you already have and less on new customers.

Further reading

Ridderstrale & Nordstrom: *Funky Business* – Chapter 4 – Funky inc.

Peter Doyle: *Value-base Marketing* – *Chapter 3*

Summary

This section looked at how to develop a Customer Relationship Management initiative and the importance of understanding your customers as part of that process, as well as planning very carefully in sufficient detail. The next section looks at how Customer Relationship Management works in practice.

III
MAKING IT HAPPEN

13

PLANNING AND IMPLEMENTING CUSTOMER RELATIONSHIP MANAGEMENT

Topics in this chapter

- 'Buy-in'
- Clarity of objectives

Syllabus topics covered

- Planning and managing Customer Relationship Management projects.

Introduction

The introduction of a Customer Relationship Management programme is not to be taken in hand lightly. It will involve major change to the organization and to its staff and the way in which data and customers are handled. It will almost certainly involve some systems change or even new systems to deliver data and will involve re-engineering the processes and training staff. It will need to be underpinned with good clear and timely communication and managed in properly to a plan. This plan will need to have been developed with adequate buy-in from the business and signed off by the executive and adequate resources allocated. Planning is crucial to success and this chapter will look at this.

The most important part of implementation is ensuring that the benefits of improved customer relationships are actually delivered. Benefits management is much more than just ensuring the high-level benefits of the business case are achieved. It is about proactively managing the regular detail of benefit delivery and associated activity in order to maintain consensus and clarity among stakeholders of the Customer Relationship Management framework.

To do this requires an understanding of the different levels of benefit to be delivered, and how they link to make up the key business case benefits of revenue, margin, cost and productivity. Increased revenue may come from increased loyalty, which may come from improved value to customers, which may come from a number of different sources, eg better products, better service, acquiring the right customers. These, in turn, may be driven by the benefits of cheaper information-gathering and staff satisfaction.

In this scheme of mutually interdependent benefits, you must understand the benefits to be delivered to customers. Customer Relationship Management is about giving benefit to get benefit (of CVP). The benefits to be delivered and their associated activities will depend on the Customer Relationship Management strategy and the drivers of customer requirements in a particular market. To calculate Customer Relationship Management benefits, data is gathered from all areas of the organization and aggregated into a benefit realization report. Subsequently the progress of benefit delivery can be monitored and measured, and remedial action taken if necessary. Changes can then be made to the Customer Relationship Management programme activities, priorities and investment. Benefits should be built into performance targets.

Figure 59: CRM programme

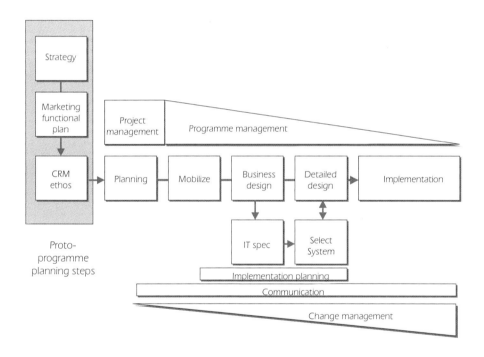

The above chart shows the key components of a Customer Relationship Management programme, which are fundamental to successful delivery and usage. Programme management is not specific to Customer Relationship Management, but is a technique particularly suited to Customer Relationship Management implementations because of its emphasis on managing change, people and different initiatives over an extensive period of time.

The basic steps as shown are:

Planning – that is preparing for the programme

Mobilization – getting the team ready and ensuring that the programme infrastructure is in place (steering committee, business staff availability, reporting protocols, logistics, rooms etc)

Business design – that is looking at what the business needs from the Customer Relationship Management programme, in the context of the proto-programme planning that has taken place.

This feeds into the **IT specification** where the systems side is developed.

Systems selection then takes place and

Detailed design is carried out of processes, structures, operating procedures, training etc.

This is all underpinned by:

- extremely active programme management
- communication (internal to the programme, upwards within the organization, and outwards) and
- change management.

During this phase the implementation planning takes place so that at the end of the phase there is a robust, well-documented plan that enables the programme to be implemented.

These are explored in detail below.

Programme management versus project management

Programme management skills are not the same as project management skills, which emphasize detailed planning. In a programme, the emphasis is on leadership, communication and benefit management — on creating the right environment for action. If Customer Relationship Management is implemented within a poorly run programme it will not improve customer value, loyalty and profitability any more than would a collection of unintegrated, disparate projects. A strong internal manager and team that understand the company are vital.

In many organizations initiatives to implement Customer Relationship Management were not coordinated adequately nor properly and as a result Customer Relationship Management was a mix of a project to implement technology coupled with some operational changes, with very little cohesion and organizational synergy. The result has ranged from outright project failure to poor or underachievement of benefit.

In a typical programme structure the programme/change management team sits between the executive steering committee, led by the Customer Relationship Management sponsor, and the project teams. The sponsor and executive steering committee oversee the programme and take responsibility for demonstrating leadership of the changes in an organizational, philosophical sense across the organization. The sponsor represents the executive steering group/board and acts as programme director, while the programme and change team organize, influence, monitor and run the implementation.

It is important to have a separation between implementing the Customer Relationship Management initiative and then managing Customer Relationship Management in practice; they are not the same and are often confused.

The former is an ad hoc project to achieve the goal of Customer Relationship Management – the latter is the day-to-day running of Customer Relationship Management, learning from the information and tweaking it to improve its performance, to track benefits and generally to monitor progress.

Organizations need to understand the gap between today and the post-Customer Relationship Management organizational vision. It is important to understand how much change is required to today's processes and cultural values as well as what other organizational changes are happening and how will they impact on this project and vice versa.

Taking a planned approach is the only way to build quickly and reap the rewards. Customer-focussed initiatives need to be identified, then managed according to their overall impact on today's processes and culture, as well as the coordination required with other business initiatives.

If the overall impact of the Customer Relationship Management vision is to improve the effectiveness of current business practices, this can be managed as a **project**. However, if the desired impact is a fundamental and strategic change to processes and culture – as most are – then a Customer Relationship Management **programme** is required.

Programme components

Any programme will have the following key inputs:

- Mission statement
- Strategic objectives
- Benefit targets
- Timetables
- Risk
- Cost objectives
- Benefits
- Scope
- Implementation
- Plan
- Business case
- Updated benefits model
- Performance measures

- Cost estimates
- Timetable estimates
- Risk indicators

These will be taken into account by the programme team and then serve as guidelines and parameters, and form a key framework for testing and validating outputs. The team will produce a document – normally called the Project Initiation Document (PID) – which will then be presented to the executive for agreement and signing off.

Customer Relationship Management is always a programme and not a project due to its far-reaching implications and will contain within its overall structure several separate but not discrete projects.

This will document all the stages and the outputs for each.

Outputs will include:

- Approach
- Scope
- Objectives
- Quantified benefit targets
- Timetables
- Implementation costs and plan
- Resources required
- Schedule
- Responsibilities
- Business cases
- Project plans
- Control and reporting
- Target benefit model
- Benefit realization mechanism and monitoring

There are four major phases to a Customer Relationship Management programme, running alongside leadership and change management.

Mobilization

This phase consists of the process of obtaining consensus to the idea and its execution. This ensures there is common agreement to the Customer Relationship Management vision and its meaning for the organization. It also ensures support for the approach and the change at the right levels. It delivers buy-in from senior management, a cross-functional programme team, and initial change management communication and actions.

Define

This part is about establishing agreement to what needs to be done for the change, as well as agreement as to the timing and manner of execution. The outputs include Customer Relationship Management capability assessment, business case, high-level outline plan (framework), objectives, and a view of costs and benefits. In this part the initial Customer Relationship Management vision is first articulated and described, with due considerations given to the trends in the industry and the external environment.

If there is no Customer Relationship Management strategy, a draft strategy is often written in this phase, or assumptions made of what the strategy is likely to be.

Key steps here include:

- validating and summarizing your business strategy
- verifying the business segments against business strategy
- agreeing customer value propositions (what need you are meeting, for whom and how your offering is differentiated) for each business segment
- determining the customer lifecycle of shared goals (interactions with mutual benefit) for each customer-value proposition
- identifying at a sufficient level of detail the activities necessary to achieve the shared goals
- deriving the key competencies (knowledge, skills and attributes) necessary to carry out the activities – these competencies are then grouped to define functionally independent logical roles
- defining the activities and responsibilities involved in the coordination of the work necessary to achieve the shared goals
- mapping the critical sets of business rules that govern the operation of the enterprise (including defining the structure of a catalogue of products and services) and which can provide competitive differentiation
- agreeing the boundaries of the overlying business processes that represent the end-to-end operation within the business segment – provides the basis for assignment of responsibility for the transition to and operation of the new enterprise
- specifying the scope of subsequent projects to produce the detailed designs of processes, information flow, skills profiles and organizational structure

Plan/Design

This is the process of designing the programme detail. The programme team is expanded and prioritizes details of the initiatives ready for execution, linking in any initiatives that have already started. Project managers are appointed. Risks, dependencies and impact are assessed (see Figure 60). Audit of data is carried out, and processes and technology reviewed. Model office is set up for business architecture details. Detailed benefits and Customer Relationship Management metrics determined. Pilots where appropriate are established.

Figure 60: Risk: Impact Assessment

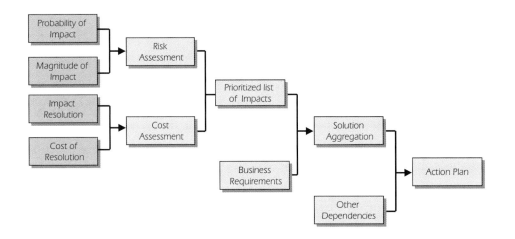

*In making the business case, the financial benefits
and risks need to be weighed*

Implementation

This phase is about the iterative execution of the programme plan, implementation of initiatives, and management of benefits. This is the most important phase in terms of delivery and thus the focus is on building Customer Relationship Management capabilities around customer interaction processes, customer insight management, technical infrastructure, skills, behaviour and organization structures.

The first stage of implementation is to gain consensus and buy-in to what Customer Relationship Management will mean to the organization for senior management. However, the problem with Customer Relationship Management is that it creates turf wars: everyone wants control of the customer and no one wants to relinquish it. The issue for the sponsor and programme team is to create the right environment for action. How to convince the board of the benefits of Customer Relationship Management is a constant question. To resolve these issues you need to:

1. Find advocates to promote Customer Relationship Management – they should act as 'Ambassadors of Progress'.

2. Establish key players' views. Do they understand Customer Relationship Management? Will they resist change? What is needed to convince them? How can you get them involved for a win-win situation?

3. Build on Customer Relationship Management benefits from known pain points, eg call centre inefficiencies, poor Web site.

4. Find innovative ways of training on Customer Relationship Management principles (video), find initiatives that demonstrate the benefits.

5. Many executives have no idea of what it is like to be a customer – have them become a customer for a day.

6. Bring customers into the organization and boardroom to tell of their experiences and views, do customer research on satisfaction and loyalty, define customers, bring them to life. This can often work best in an informal way.

7. Demonstrate what competitors and other enterprises are doing to improve their Customer Relationship Management.

Change management and communication should be run as a separate phase. The pace and frenzy of Customer Relationship Management implementations often means communication is ad hoc and ineffective. Lack of attention to communicating the benefits of Customer Relationship Management throughout an organization will allow resistance to develop and perhaps even threaten the programme. At best, this slows things down; at worst, it threatens success. Successful Customer Relationship Management requires major changes in staff attitude, behaviour and culture.

On average, it takes two years for new behaviours to replace the old – further delays to this momentum should be minimized. Organizations need to move from customer-aware but fragmented cultures, to more team-oriented and customer-intimate cultures, and eventually to customer-centric cultures, where behaviour is based on building customer loyalty. Change requires the commitment of all staff – they need to know what is in it for them or they will revert to old ways. Their reward/remuneration must be linked to the new, changed way of working. The same techniques that work with the Board can be adapted to work for the whole organization. In this case however:

1. The resource required will be greater, and budget needs to be approved for it.

2. Impact mapping may be required to establish the different groups affected and the changes in behaviour required.

3. Communication needs planning through phases to create awareness, demonstrate benefits, ensure everyone knows their place in relation to customers, and be continuously educated in customer expectations.

4. Continuous coaching and reinforcement for the new behaviour needed in the organization will be required.

5. Behaviours and staff satisfaction and attitude the change must be measured and monitored to check change is on track, to highlight deviations or threats and to enable connective action to be taken.

How not to do it

There are 12 key commandments for implementing a programme badly:

- do not set up the implementation programme in good time

- treat it as a tactical issue only

- treat it as an IT issue only

- fail to budget adequately for the work required

- ignore your customers' needs

- ignore what your competitors are doing

- skimp on the business impact assessment

- skimp on the operational impact assessment

- leave impact assessment to individual business units

- leave implementation to individual business units

- fail to appreciate the scale of executive involvement in decision making

- fail to understand the training implications

Key learning points

1. Clarity of objectives is critical.

2. Customer Relationship Management is a programme not a series of separate projects.

3. Strong management coupled with user sponsorship and support is vital to success.

4. Timings for implementation must be realistic.

Further reading

Russell-Jones: *Project Management Pocketbook*

14

THE ROLE OF THE RELATIONSHIP MANAGER

Topics in this chapter

- What a relationship manager does
- Why he is different from an ordinary employee
- Characteristics of a relationship manager

Syllabus topics covered

- Building relationships.
- Managing customer relationships.
- Time management.

Introduction

For Customer Relationship Management to be successful a change in culture attitudes and the way of dealing with customers is required. One of these changes is the use of relationship managers. Their sole focus is on managing customers to ensure that they place as much of their business with you as possible. Obviously not all customers will warrant their own individual managers and equally they will spend differing amounts of time on customers. They are, however, a key element in successful Customer Relationship Management.

14.1   What is a relationship manager?

This is a role that may be more likely to be a set of activities that comprise the universe of relationship managers' activities than a specific role although perhaps for corporate clients it is much more likely to be defined. Often the role is unclear or has been established based on a false premise:

Clients say:

'I want 'personalized service' and 'close personal attention to company needs'.

This is often interpreted as:

'One person must be sole provider of services'

which leads to an impossible role for the manager.

The true interpretation should be that:

The relationship manager serves as the focus for client needs and the channel for service provision.

14.2   Why have they not always been effective?

The concept of a relationship manager is not a new one, however, the impetus from competition and, therefore, a greater need to manage relationships through the aegis of a Customer Relationship Management initiative has resurrected the idea. In the past, however, they have not always been as successful as was hoped. Analysis of relationships managers revealed that too often they spend the majority (80%) of their time on non-revenue related activities – a classic Pareto inversion – and only 20% on revenue generation. Clearly these two should be the other way round to stop them from being expensive administrators and filing clerks.

Figure 61: RMs – Too busy for customers

Activity analysis reveals poor use of time.
75% is non-revenue related – they are expensive clerks with poor time management

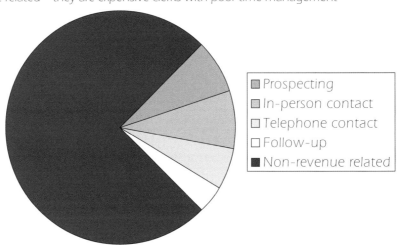

Source: BBB Research

There are a number of reasons why some managers have been ineffective – these include many authorization processes which are inefficient/bureaucratic. There are three key processes in relationship management:

Sales

- usually insufficiently focused
- tasks to achieve sales goals not carried out well
- emphasis on new business 'hunting' rather than 'farming' existing client base
- cross-disciplinary efforts poor
- organizations' talents underutilized

Authorization/Credit

Is often very expensive. Typical symptoms:

- slow approvals
- poor credit quality
- declining efficiency
- low levels of productive automation
- too many hand-offs

IBM Credit Corp, the finance arm of IBM, re-engineered its loan processing system and changed the turnaround from ten days to six hours

Administration

Usually too much effort is wasted prior to the decision with form filling or unnecessary data collection. Analysis of such processes has shown that up to 80% of activities in some processes represents wasted or non-value added time

- poor usage of Customer Relationship Management systems
  - Managers need the right information at the right time to enable them to carry out their duties effectively (market, client, profit/costs)
  - MIS has been often ill-suited to real needs – and usually driven by history, system constraints (real or imagined) and poor user involvement in establishing the MIS
  - There has usually been poor sales tracking and other information
  - Garbage in garbage out (GIGO) holds true here
- too many people in the chain, with poorly-defined responsibilities

- menial tasks are often insufficiently delegated

- support is often poor:

  - most common to have administration assistants supporting relationship managers

  - this has caused issues because they carry out only low-level tasks, thus requiring the RM to spend too much time on non-revenue generating activities

The use of assistant relationship managers instead of administrative assistants has led to up to 40% freeing of relationship managers time from non-revenue activities. They are also more able to solve customer problems than administrative assistants, and it provides a training ground for future relationship managers.

Given their role, however, relationship managers should be able to demonstrate effective value generation to an organization. By judicious usage of the Customer Relationship Management that supports them they can re-focus their time and increasingly will generate business and more importantly an increasing share of customers' wallets.

Relationship managers in general have a better understanding of the buying process of their customers. In addition they:

- make better use of internal resources – ie they know how to use and where to get information, they talk to the right colleagues who are able to give them the knowledge or information that they need to meet customer needs – networking across an organization is vital

- monitor their own activity more closely and understand where the down time is and how they spend their day and adjust activity accordingly

- have sharper focused call objectives – single point or realistic

- adopt momentum sales plans

- plan sales goals

- use 'sales funnels' and manage them actively

- use cross-disciplinary skills where relevant

- delegate non-revenue tasks to other, more junior staff

- focus on the buying cycle of an individual or an organization and in the latter case understand who are decision-makers and personnel with real buying powers

- track clients and build relationships

14.3   Some myths about relationship managers

The folklore surrounding successful relationship managers usually asserts that they have the following characteristics:

- curious
- aggressive
- charismatic
- extroverted
- ambitious
- persistent
- focused
- high-energy

Research, however, shows a wholly different set of characteristics of relationship managers in that they:

- set goals for themselves
- plan their days, weeks, months
- delegate administration work
- analyse the buying process
- never prospect without referral
- work fewer prospects harder – and, therefore, particularly lend themselves to a Customer Relationship Management initiative

> 'We want to be regarded as the premier financial services firm bringing value-added products to a limited group of major customers'
>
> Bob Engel: J P Morgan

Why they are different from other employees

Relationship managers have specific roles to fulfill within an organization. This is about managing the relationship rather than (usually) in delivering. Their objectives are to increase the organization's share of the customer's wallet. To this end they require a different set of **Knowledge**, **Skills** and **Attributes** from ordinary employees to be successful, including:

Knowledge

- Products – implications and requirements for success
- Organization – structure, cross-organizational issues
- Customers' needs and wants

Skills

- Negotiation
- Listening
- Decision-making

Attributes

- Numerate – to understand cashflows, NPVs and some complex products, depending on role
- Literate – able to write letters, develop presentations and write reports
- Presentable – so that the customers are comfortable with him in one-to-ones but also as a face of the organization
- Consistent – the same message to customers in the same way
- Able to put across complex issues in an easy format
- Focus (80% on existing customers – 20% on new)

14.4　Prioritizing time

It is vital that the time you have available is used in the most efficient and effective manner (efficient is doing things in the best way possible – effective is doing things that are focused on what you want to achieve.) To do this it is necessary to understand what you do and why you do it. Then you need to categorize activities into four areas :

- first by timing and whether they need short-term or longer-term action
- second by type of activity response – whether they are initiated by you – proactive – or whether they come to you for action – reactive
- third as to whether they are urgent
- fourth as to whether they are important.

NB you need to understand the difference between the latter two – and also that tasks can be both urgent **and** important.

A simple 2 X 2 grid can help here as shown below. Here tasks are split into **Timing** versus **Type of response** and can then be marked to indicate importance or urgency.

Figure 62: Task/activity prioritization

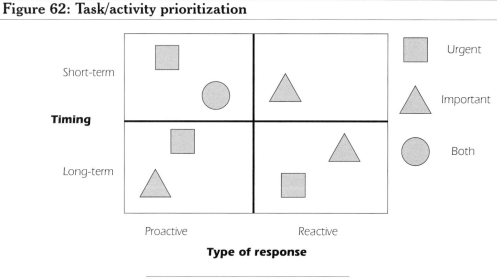

This allows you to expend the right amount of effort on the key tasks. Note that some activities can become urgent if you leave them too long!

One of the key skills for relationship managers is customer handling. (see below).

Skills

Relationship managers need different skills from other employees. Within most organizations staff usually have a functional specialism and sometimes a little knowledge of other areas. These are known as 'I' shaped (deep knowledge in one area) and 'T' shaped staff (deep knowledge in one area and a smattering of knowledge across the top). In order for Customer Relationship Management to work smoothly staff in general and relationship managers in particular need to acquire a broader and at the same time deeper set of skills and understanding of products and organizational capability known as 'Y' shaped. The diagram shows this.

Figure 63: Staff skills metamorphosis required

Typical organization – largely functional specialist

New CRM-focused organization with many staff having broad product knowledge

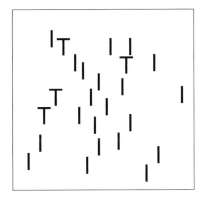 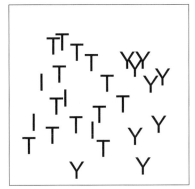

To achieve CRM the organization needs to migrate its staff competencies from largely 'I' with some 'T': to largely 'T' with many 'Y'

For an organization this will necessitate:

● Ensuring the right staff fill the roles

● That relationship managers have the right training

● That product knowledge is sufficient

● That they understand the breadth of the organization's capabilities

● If necessary recruiting (novation)

● That remuneration levels and form is right to drive and set the new behaviours.

Key learning points

1. Relationship managers have specific roles to fulfill within an organization. This is about managing the relationship rather than (usually) in delivering. Their objectives are to increase the organization's share of the customer's wallet.

2. Time management is critical – as is a focus on existing customers – 'farming'.

3. The organization needs to ensure that it has the right calibre of staff with the right skills and in-depth product knowledge.

Further reading

F Reichheld: *Loyalty Rules*

Langdon: *Key Accounts are Different*

15

CHANGE MANAGEMENT

Topics in this chapter

● New processes

● Changing behaviours

● Incentivizing staff

Syllabus topics covered

● Managing customer communications.

● Planning and managing Customer Relationship Management projects.

Introduction

'Change management is now "business as usual" for us'

Director – UK Life Insurance co.

What is meant by change management? It is simply this: the process of moving from the current state to the 'vision' of the future and it involves a transition which may involve some pain for some or, more commonly, most. It is about introducing the new operating mechanisms in an organization that will ensure that the required behaviours are implemented and that they are maintained.

Figure 64: Change management

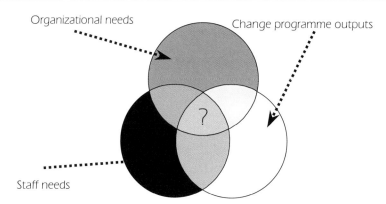

The more closely aligned these three are – the more
likely you are to succeed

Change involves moving an organization's:

● people and

● culture

into line with an organization's new

● strategy

● structure

● processes and

● systems.

There are some key statements about change:

● It is very difficult

● The further you go the harder it becomes

● The less that the change has in common with the organization's culture then the less
likely it is to succeed (this does not mean that you cannot change a culture but that you
must build on the strengths or the aspects that will support the new desired position)

● It needs strong sponsorship

● Goals must be absolutely clear for all stakeholders

● A body of people dedicated to making it happen is essential

● Communication is key

As a result it does need strong management – it will not 'just happen' if it is left alone. It
requires a dedicated resource that will have some clear objectives:

- To ensure that there is a shared vision across the organization as to what precisely the change means at the macro – organizational – level and also for individuals

- To analyse the organization from a change perspective to understand its own unique characteristics and the areas that will require special attention

- To try to ensure that change is made in ways that dovetail with the 'cultural norms and mores'

- To communicate

- To lead the project and manage it

- To ensure buy-in from stakeholders (who will include employees, management, customers, shareholders and possibly local communities and government)

There are two areas that will hinder what they do:

Culture – how an organization operates. The project will almost certainly be counter-cultural in some or more ways and the organization will 'kick' against the change. The team will need to analyse the culture and understand how it operates. Do not underestimate the strength of culture – it can have serious impacts on a programme and defeat it. It is intangible but is a blend of several features:

- History – how things have been done in the past

- Ownership (PLC; mutual; single ownership; family; employee; state; partnership; cooperative)

- Operating environment – global; international; regional; local; branch-based or multi-channel

- Its mission and goals, which shape what it does

- The type of people or the mix and dominant forces – graduates, school leavers, actuarial, accountants, sales

Culture is an ever changing animal[22]. *Culture shouldn't be used as an excuse for not moving ahead in a changing environment. Part of our culture is to stay ahead. Some items will remain forever – like integrity and loyalty to our people and clients.*

Hilmar Kopper – Deutsche Bank

People – how people react individually to change. Those affected adversely will obviously need to be identified but so too will those affected positively or neutrally. Almost everyone reacts negatively to change. This is due to human nature which appears to be generally opposed to anything that alters the status quo.

There are two types of reaction to change, negative and positive; however, both sets of people go through what could be classed as a difficult time – the difference is how soon they emerge at the other end.

[22] Quoted in Steven I Davis: *Managing Change in Excellent Banks* (Macmillan 1989)

Negative reaction involves the following steps (often described as similar to grieving for a loved one):

- Immobilization where they are in shock
- Denial of the change
- Anger at the change
- Bargaining to try to alter it
- Depression as a result of it
- Testing to absorb it
- Acceptance of the change (this latter assumes that they make it through).

For those taking it positively:

- Uninformed optimism – where they are self-confident and positive to the change
- Informed pessimism – where they start exhibiting negative responses to the change
- Hopeful realism – where they see the achievability of the change and confidence grows
- Informed optimism – confidence returns and they throw themselves into the project
- Completion – where they act as ambassadors of progress and give out confidence.

Different people react in different ways and with different timescales. It is this aspect that must be managed.

Making change happen

A US survey[23] found that the most common causes of failure were:

- Employee resistance
- Inappropriate culture
- Poor communication/plan
- Incomplete follow-up
- Insufficient skills

Communication

This is critical to change. It is about informing all the right parties at the right time.

Key questions are:

- Who should be told?
- When should they be told?
- How much should they be told?

[23] William Schliemann and Associates Inc

- How should you convey the message?

It is vital that in implementing such a far-reaching and fundamentally different programme as Customer Relationship Management that the right communication is given – as it is for any major project. Failure will result in misunderstandings, misinformation and issues arising unnecessarily.

Leadership

Another important aspect of change is leadership – both of the programme and in influencing the organization. Customer Relationship Management is a very important aspect of an organization's business and managing in the change must be successful. The programme needs to build up credibility quickly and to maintain it. As such the leader is critical.

Figure 65: Leadership elements

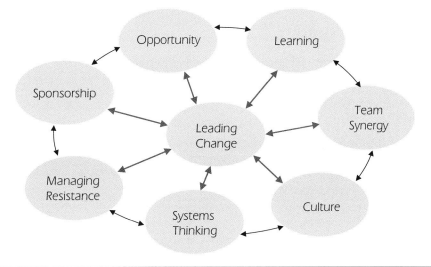

Leadership is not the same as management and is about:

- Vision
- Inspiration
- Honesty
- Credibility
- Communication
- DWYSYWD
- Trust
- Belief

Management on the other hand is about:

- Goals

- Expectations

- Rewards

- Feedback

- Teams

- Delegation

- Empowerment

- Deliverables

Not all managers make good leaders – and vice versa. It is important, therefore, that both roles are clear and that the right individuals take the right roles.

15.1   Incentivizing staff

One of the key components of Customer Relationship Management is that it usually demands a different set of incentives from the norm. This is best linked to a series of competency assessments where reward is linked to outputs and results.

If competence is what the relationship manager puts into a job, then results are the outputs. This may seem a simple observation to make, but generally organizations place the emphasis on rewarding results without considering that it might achieve the same or better results by investing in people's inputs.

At a management level, companies frequently point to the usefulness of competency frameworks in equipping line managers to perform their people-management function more effectively. Competencies give managers the tools to understand the performance levels expected from their direct reports, how these can be measured and what needs to be done in the way of coaching, training and development to remedy any shortfalls. At the level of the individual employee, the benefit of competencies will be to provide role clarity, so that individuals are clearer about the demands of the job and what behaviours are paramount.

Using competencies allows the organization and the relationship managers the means to improve sales performance by focusing in a systematic way on those skills that will give your business a competitive edge and greater than average returns. Without this structured approach it is difficult to address the hidden costs that make running a sales force (or relationship management team) so expensive:

- poor, unskilled recruitment, resulting in people with substandard skills being brought on board;

- failure to recognize the psychological contract and the implicit bargain between competence and recognition, leading to people feeling undervalued and de-motivated;

- blunt incentives which incentivize people at high cost to achieve a narrow range of results at the cost of colleagues and the customer;
- poor training, coaching and development which fail to address real competence shortcomings;
- salespeople who fail to live up to your brand image and the promise of good service and advice;
- managers who are unable to manage.

The results of ignoring the people dimension include:

- high staff turnover
- unfocused training
- poor motivation
- inadequate and wasted incentives
- unskilled recruitment
- poor fitting values
- marred brand reputation

Key learning points

1. Implementing change is difficult and needs a strong focus.
2. Leadership is a critical factor – along with management – and the two are different.
3. Culture must be understood and change aligned as much as possible.
4. Staff must be incentivized to follow the new Customer Relationship Management way of doing business.
5. People must be managed through the change because they are the most likely barriers to success.

Further reading

Russell-Jones: *Change Management Pocketbook*

Elisabeth Moss-Kantor: *Teaching Elephants to Dance*

Ridderstrale and Nordstrom: *Funky Business*

16

Customer Relationship Management in Practice

Topics in this chapter

- Organizational decision-making

- Preparing presentations

Syllabus topics covered

- Organizational buying behaviour.

- Understanding and managing customer expectations.

- Building relationships by adding value to customers cost-effectively.

- Understanding and evaluating customer business plans.

- Effective interviews with customers.

- Analysis and evaluation of information: identifying business opportunities.

- Preparing proposals for customers.

Introduction

The practicalities of Customer Relationship Management involve dealing with the customers daily. This is different from theory and is never quite like the handbooks. This is because customers are different from each other and do not conform to stereotypes. You have to make the best of it. This means understanding them and their needs, and formulating solutions to their needs, as referred to previously. It also means managing their expectations – you cannot always offer them what they want – and they have to understand that, as well as the fact that they have to pay for service. It is far harder to deal with organizations and, therefore, this topic is dealt with here in some detail. Also one of the major items for relationship managers is presenting proposals.

16.1   Organizational decision-making

Dealing with organizations is very different from dealing with individuals.

It is very rare that important or critical decisions are taken by one person. Usually several people are involved, whether through a hierarchical process (eg in many Japanese companies) or in a group/team or committee.

Group dynamics are different from individual dynamics and need to be understood. This is because each member of the group will have group objectives but will also have his or her own agenda – his or her own goals and characteristics.

To manage corporate customers effectively you need to understand all of those involved in the buying process – or at least those key decision-makers and influencers – and you must understand each individual's personal goals in terms of:

- **logic**
- **politics**
- **emotion**

To obtain a decision from a group it is necessary to understand not only the **logical** argument that will convince each of the key individuals that the decision will be the right one, but also the **emotional** arguments (what do I get out of this?) and their **political** aims (will this make me look good in the organization or among my peers and superiors?).

Each one will ask him or herself What is in this for me? How can this advance my personal ambition or my status within the group/organization? Failure to meet their needs will result in their rejection of the decision – either overtly – where at least it can be dealt with, or more likely and probably more damaging, covertly, where they will oppose it without saying so.

In group situations you must carry a majority of the group or at least the key decision-makers who will outvote the rest or 'force' the decision. A typical example of this is in consulting where, before presentation of findings on an assignment, consultants will 'pre-present' findings to individuals separately and try to deal with their objections in isolation, rather than within a plenary forum where it could lead to damaging arguments.

The diagram overleaf shows the importance of these three aspects. The more closely you can align your offering to the centre where it hits all three aspects the more likely you are to succeed. Often great focus is placed on the business case (logic) and the other aspects are overlooked or given insufficient attention.

Figure 66: Group dynamics

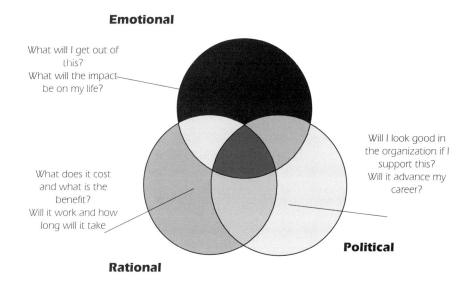

Emotional

What will I get out of this?
What will the impact be on my life?

Will I look good in the organization if I support this?
Will it advance my career?

What does it cost and what is the benefit?
Will it work and how long will it take

Political

Rational

16.2   Structuring your argument

To persuade others to support your decision or to lead them into taking the decision that you wish them to take, you must structure your argument so well that it leads them step by step to the inescapable, logical conclusion. That is the same conclusion that you have reached and to which you are now asking them to agree. The way to do this is to lead them to your conclusions without them realizing it.

This is done by setting out:

● what is common knowledge

● the situation

● the issue – the complication, or what is wrong

● then the decision that is required

So far they cannot disagree because you are re-stating facts that should be known and understood.

Then you set out:

● the conclusion that is the decision

● then the supporting evidence.

Faced with such a logical approach most people will readily come to the same conclusions as you and agree with your analysis and accept the logic (you may of course not meet the other (political and emotional) issues so they need to be factored into the argument as well). The argument must of course be constructed logically and contain no flaws.

16.3   Service recovery

No matter how good your Customer Relationship Management programme, mistakes and errors will occur. The financial services sector is heavily reliant on people and as a result there is a high propensity for errors to occur wherever there is a human interface. Good procedures and training will go a long way to minimizing this but nevertheless they will still happen. One of the hallmarks of an excellent organization is how it deals with these errors when they do happen. They should be viewed as learning experiences and used to illustrate what needs to be done – as well as taking steps to fix them.

Complaints cost you money – from two sources: the cost of rectification – which usually increases with time – and the potential business lost from the complainant. It is important, therefore, to ensure that complaints are handled quickly but sensibly.

Case study: Building Society

A building society had a policy of investigating all phantom withdrawals from ATMs. This was to ensure that customers' complaints were dealt with adequately. It was slow and in the majority of cases the withdrawals were found to be false or internal errors. Money was only repaid at the end of the process. Customers were highly dissatisfied with the process and as well as complaining about the withdrawals were complaining about the delays in fixing them. The process was reviewed and not only was the dissatisfaction found to be very high but it was very expensive to carry out the checks. As a result a new policy adopted of paying out on all claims immediately with subsequent investigation – where necessary (as many resolved themselves subsequently) with the proviso that where more than a set number occurred (3) within a given period then they would not be recompensed until they were investigated fully. This greatly improved customer handling and also enabled staff to get on with day-to-day operations without constant queries and complaints about the process.

Organizations that have examined their complaints-handling process have usually developed a new set of procedures with one or two key paradigms – resolution should take place as near to the customer as possible – and as quickly as possible. This is supported by an escalation process which is transparent to the customer so that they can have the confidence that any complaints will be taken seriously.

Complaints should of course be recorded and that data fed into the database to allow patterns of issues to be identified and subsequently resolved.

Dealing with complaints is a skill that not everybody has. There are some key issues that are helpful.

Do:

- give your name
- let the person decide if they wish to pursue their 'complaint' as a complaint
- tell the person what will happen next and the stages of the procedure
- get their details, eg names, addresses, telephone numbers, dates
- get the facts/make notes
- listen
- accept complaints even if they are not about your section/department
- stay calm even if the person gets angry
- be sympathetic
- take the person seriously
- be honest
- let the person have their say
- act quickly once the complainant has left

Do not:

- argue with the complainant
- get angry
- get into a blame conversation
- undermine the organization
- pass the complainant on to someone else
- accept abuse from a complainant, eg swearing
- ask them to complain in writing or in person or come back later
- deter people from making a complaint
- consider the complaint as a personal criticism
- use jargon when writing back to the complainant

Dealing with complaints is quite normal – but of course action should be taken to minimize them.

Case study: UCI[24]

UCI is a major cinema operator. It deals with 80 million customers annually in the UK alone – as well as operating overseas – and found it difficult to keep track of them all. It was also dealing with complaints on an individual basis and missing the big picture. It installed a new complaints-handling system as part of Customer Relationship Management into its cinemas and found it was able to identify key issues such as popcorn packets leaking and thus causing it to pay for dry cleaning. Changing the bags saved it a fortune. The new process also allows them to filter out 'persistent or professional complainers' and thus save time and money.

Corporate responses to complaints data

Once a complaint has been dealt with – and hopefully resolved – the details should of course be captured in a complaints log. The organization needs to review this periodically for recurrences and major issues and costs. While it is true that one complaint represents several and several may represent very many – it is not always so and it does not mean that the entire customer base is unhappy.

The complaints may be representative of only the feelings of an isolated individual or a small group of customers. You cannot please everyone all of the time and you are probably pleasing most customers (who you do not hear from). You do not have to change your policies to accommodate a few customers – especially where it is outside of your CVP.

Case study: South West Airlines

South West Airlines, which pioneered low-cost flights, started out operating in Texas, USA. They flew only between towns in the state of Texas and offered no frills and very cheap flights. Each year they receive many complaints from passengers who want, inter alia, food served on the flight, the ability to check in baggage to other airlines, allocated seating and so on. South West does not change its policy because of these complaints as its stated policy is not to offer these things. That is why its flights are so cheap as it does not have to ticket baggage, wait for flights to come in etc. Those sort of complaints are outside of its CVP and so it does not address them. Of course a complaint about staff or other relevant areas would be addressed.

It is important to make this distinction before making changes in response to a complaint. Once you have determined that a complaint that recurs is serious, however, then you must address it immediately and make the necessary changes.

Negative customer feedback and complaints should always be viewed as an opportunity for improvement. The serious evaluation of customer complaints and questions is a necessary and effective way of learning from mistakes, and ultimately enabling you to increase sales by taking action whether to resolve an error – customer satisfaction increases dramatically after a successful resolution of an error – or by obviating future occurrences.

[24] See (9).

Here are some extracts from organizations' websites on complaints. These have been chosen at random and do not necessarily contain all detail. Note that for some organizations not listed here it was difficult to find the right section and that in general it is harder to find out from insurance companies' websites, indicating that they have not quite thought this issue through.

Barclays

Complaints Commitment

Don't hold back your feedback. We are committed to providing a high standard of service to you and all our customers. Occasionally we may not live up to our promises. If this happens, we want to hear from you. Letting us know when you are unhappy with the service you experience gives us the opportunity to put matters right for you and to improve our service in the future for everybody...

...Sometimes we may not be able to sort it out straight away. Where we cannot resolve it by the following day, this is what you can expect from us:

- A written acknowledgement of your complaint within five working days.

- Details of who is handling your complaint and how to contact them. Sometimes this may not be the person who received your complaint but the individual best placed to deal with it.

- If your complaint will take longer to investigate, we will keep you informed of progress.

- We aim to resolve your complaint within four weeks. If we are unable to do so, we will write explaining what's happening and let you know when we expect to do so.

- After eight weeks we will send you a final response or a further progress report on our investigations.

If you are still not happy...

Our aim is to resolve your complaint as quickly as possible and to your complete satisfaction. If, for whatever reason, you are unhappy with the response you receive from us please get in touch directly with the person or department who handled your complaint. They will then agree with you what the next steps are.

If you are still dissatisfied, you can request a review from the Financial Ombudsman Service.

Lloyds/TSB

Voicing your concern

We want to put things right as quickly as possible, so we've set up a 3-step procedure to resolve your complaints.

Step 1: approach your usual point of contact. You'll need:

● your full name and address

● full details of your complaint

● your account number, branch sort code and any policy numbers (do not include this information if you are contacting us by e-mail)

● what you think we should do to put things right

● photocopies of any relevant paperwork

We always aim to resolve your complaint at this stage.

Step 2: refer to a complaint support unit

● If you are not satisfied with our response, we may refer you on to an appropriate manager or department for further investigation.

Step 3: ask the support unit to issue you with a 'final response'

● If your complaint has not been resolved to your satisfaction, we will give you a 'final response'. This outlines your complaint and our response. We'll also provide you with details of the Financial Ombudsman Service.

If we haven't sent you a final response within 8 weeks of first raising the complaint, you may approach the Financial Ombudsman Service directly.

Halifax

Stage 1 – Where you first make your complaint

We aim to resolve your concerns within 24 hours. Sometimes it may take longer to look into the matter fully. If this happens, we will let you know within 5 working days, who will reply.

Often the people you first raise the matter with are able to help, but there may be occasions when it needs a specialist area to be involved. If you don't know who to contact you can:

telephone Customer Relations on:

0845 600 8000

or a textphone is available for you if you have a hearing impairment on:

0845 600 1750

write to us at:

Halifax plc
Halifax Customer Relations
Trinity Road
Halifax HX1 2RG

We will then arrange for the right person to look into and respond to your concerns.

Stage 2 – Customer Relations

In the unlikely event that you remain unhappy, you can ask for your complaint to be referred to a Customer Relations manager for further review. If you are still not satisfied you can, at this stage, ask the Financial Ombudsman Service to help, or for service-related complaints about Halifax Estate Agencies Limited, the Ombudsman for Estate Agents.

The Halifax supports fully and is a member of both the Ombudsman Schemes. These are impartial and conduct independent investigations.

16.4 Preparing presentations

It is a frequent occurrence that you will be forced to make a presentation to your customers. This may be of several types:

- In plenary session to many customers

- To a small group from a corporate customer

- To an individual either in her private capacity or perhaps as a representative of a corporate.

Although they are all different in one way given the nature of the event and the audience and you must tailor your presentation to that – in essence there are a few rules that apply to any presentation and the following questions should always be your frame of reference when considering and preparing a presentation:

- What are your objectives?

- How long do you have/need?

- Where will it take place?

- What media will you be using?

- Who is the audience?

- What should the content be?

- How will you structure it?

- How long will it take to put together?

Remember that a presentation is like an iceberg – 90% is unseen (below the water-line) and is in the planning and preparation. The delivery, although important, is only the tip.

Below these are explored in detail.

What are your objectives

Why are you making the presentation in the first place? You should be extremely clear as to why you are doing this. Is it to explain about your product? Is it to explain a new structure that is being put in place for customers? Are you asking them for a decision? If so is the objective:

- clear
- have all options been identified
- has data been gathered to support the analysis
- has the analysis been carried out and a brief prepared explaining:
  - the impact from each option
  - the risk of the option
  - the likelihood of the risk occurring
  - the cost of doing it
  - the implications of not doing it
  - timing

Unless you have the answers to these questions then your audience will not be clear as to why they are making the decision and, therefore, they cannot hope to make the right one, nor to understand the real drivers of the need to make the decision. Accordingly either you will not achieve the desired result or you will get a partial or incorrect decision.

How long do you have/need?

The time that you have been allocated is critical – either you will have to cut the presentation to fit in with the time or you need to ask for longer – but be sure that you have a good reason and a good argument for so doing. Note that the type of media used affects the timings – a series of power-point/freelance slides with builds can take much longer to get through than paper handouts of the same thing when talked through informally round a table.

Where will it take place?

This will affect what you can say, and how you say it. Presenting in a plenary session is different from a small group and different again from a intimate one-to-one. If you choose to use electronic media then you should really check the venue for what is available and to make sure everything is compatible and works (is their software OK, is there a spare bulb for the OHP, can you link into the Lite-pro with your PC? Are the acoustics all right – what is the configuration of the room – are the seats OK – is it right for a presentation or an informal talk through etc. There is nothing worse than turning up with a PC presentation to be presented with a battered OHP.

What media will you be using?

(Paper, OHP, powerpoint/freelance slides etc.) The media should be chosen to suit the type of meeting and also what is easily available. It is clearly inappropriate to use paper handouts for a large group – apart from anything else using the wrong media looks unprofessional, especially if they are used to receiving presentations.

Who is the audience?

This is critical. If you are looking for a decision then unless the decision-maker(s) are present you are wasting your time. Knowing who will be there is the first step – of more use is knowing their own agendas and objectives. Any personal information you have will also pay dividends when you engage in the small talk or relate an answer to a question to their own particular circumstances.

What should the content be?

Clearly the content must support the objectives. It should be presented in a logical flow to lead the listeners to your conclusion and to ensure that the message has been put across.

It is often useful to leave paper printouts of any presentations behind – or even to give them out in advance so that they can follow what you are saying and make notes as they go along. Depending on what is in it you might want to give them an 'edited' version if confidential information is involved.

What actions (research etc) do you need to put in hand to obtain the information that you need in the presentation – how long will it take – where should you go to get it – do you need help?

If possible tailor any information to the audience. If giving examples make sure that they are relevant and reinforce the points that you wish to make in their context. It is pointless referring analogously to a situation in a global oil company's operations in the Middle East when talking to a small manufacturer of socks – unless there is a very useful lesson or parallel that makes a good point. Similarly it is of little value talking about equity release to a first-time buyer.

How will you structure it?

The structure is important and here it is very useful to remember the old adage

KISS – Keep It Simple Stupid

It should contain the following – without exception!

- An introduction to you and the session, as well as to the objectives of the presentation (yours and theirs). If appropriate they can also introduce themselves briefly

- An agenda containing the details of what you are going to cover

- A short background section if appropriate

- An executive summary of the key points

- The detail

- A summary of what you have said and conclusions if appropriate

- Next steps if appropriate

- Close and questions

Prior to presenting get someone else to look at it critically – does everything you have put on it pass the 'so what?' test?

Logic in structure

Use the following template developed by Barbara Minto[25] to get arguments across. It uses logic and understanding of people's thought processes to order information logically to persuade them to agree to the decision (that you require).

First describe the **Situation**

Then the **Complication** (what we do not like about it)

Then the **Question** you are trying to answer

Then the **Answer** to the question

The first three points should be familiar to the audience already because they form the basis of the presentation. You then give them the answer and support it with facts and they are already most of the way there to agreeing.

For example:

You are a company that manufactures xx **(situation)**

You have received a major order from overseas that requires a major investment in working capital **(complication)**

How shall this be financed? **(question)**

We can provide you with O/D, export finance, foreign exchange contracts, letters of credit etc **(answer).**

This is then followed by facts and figures etc supporting the answer and demonstrating why it is a good answer and that they should agree.

[25] Barbara Minto: *Pyramid Thinking* (Pitman)

General points

DO

- Ask if they can hear you and can see clearly

- Use diagrams to illustrate points – but make them simple. For complex diagrams (and if it is appropriate) build them up

- Explain diagrams and tables – and give them time to absorb them

- Get your numbers right – it destroys credibility if there are errors in a presentation

- Welcome people and thank them for attending – at the beginning and at the end

- Think of the presentation from the audience's perception – what are their frames of reference – what will they understand?

- Make lots of eye contact – critical – do not look at your notes and read them out

- Face the audience – but have good movement

- Make it lively – use different voice tones and nuances – inject humour where you can and if appropriate

- Project to the back of the hall

- Rehearse – especially if you are unfamiliar with presenting

- Refer questions to colleagues if they are present – but do not give them 'hospital passes'

- Where appropriate, ask the audience to answer a question from another participant

- Try to make it as interactive as possible either by asking questions instead of making statements or using them in the presentation to confirm points etc

- Take supporting documentation with you if appropriate

DO NOT

- put too many points on a slide. Around five or six is acceptable – but be sensible – if you need eight points on one slide then put them on but make them easy to understand

- use jargon – or if you do then explain unfamiliar terms or abbreviations

- mumble

- speak too fast

- fiddle with things in your pocket

- be nervous (easy to say)

- play with objects in your hands (pens, pointers etc) – put them down if you are not using them

- talk down to the audience – eg '…it is perfectly clear that…' '…or it is obvious that…' – it may not be to them

- ignore questions – answer them, and ask if you have answered the question

- give an inadequate answer – say rather that you will get back to them – and do so

How long will it take to put together?

When planning a presentation it is useful to consider how long it night take to prepare. It can take a long time to research and then prepare presentations. Setting timescales and resource limits can help enormously.

16.5   Effective customer meetings

Although interview techniques have been discussed earlier there are some other useful issues for consideration. To make meetings or interviews truly effective then you must conduct them properly. This means understanding the nature of human interactions. People operate on three levels in meetings[26] – they are called:

- Chatter

- Intellectual

- Emotional

Understanding these three levels and the differences between them is important – because moving into the wrong style can close down a meeting before it has even started.

Chatter is the meaningless talk that just fills time – eg 'how are you?' – 'did you see the game last night?' – 'did you have a good trip up?' – 'would you like a cup of tea?' etc. We do it unconsciously all the time but it is an important non-threatening way to start off a meeting. This phase is a very important part of creating the environment where the customer feels at ease and is willing to talk. You then gradually move into the next phase.

Intellectual is the phase where questions cause the respondent to think about his answer and develops mutual understanding of the objectives and ultimately a resolution. Good meetings should never pass beyond this phase. Unfortunately many do and often very quickly move into the third phase.

Emotion – is where the respondent starts to feel very uncomfortable with the questions as they feel that they are being pressurized or that you are asking the wrong, irrelevant or personal questions. This has only one ending – the customer is unhappy. 'Hard' selling often ends up here.

The diagram shows the three types of questioning. The best types of meeting never progress beyond the intellectual phase. In meeting 1 it has quickly progressed into emotion, (an interrogation). In 2, while the meeting started off well, it gradually slipped up into the emotional area – ie the questioner went too far. Number 3 is a well-structured and well-run meeting that will achieve its objectives. Note – too much chatter can result in not getting to the point!

[26] Dwight S Ritter: *Relationship Banking* (Bankers Publishing Company – Chicago USA)

Figure 67: Questioning intensity curves

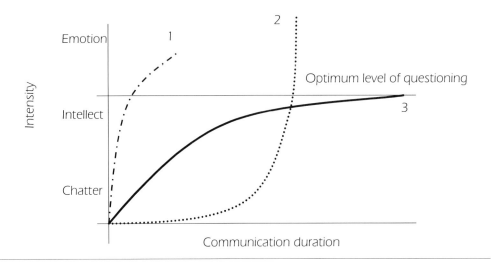

Imparting difficult messages

Some meetings of course have different objectives – for example, where you need to close an account or let a customer know that his facilities will not be made available. These require just as careful handling although perhaps a little more firmness is needed. Any organization that is managing its customers for value will have to manage out the accounts that do not fit with its profitability profile. There is no difference in handling the meetings except that you must be even more careful not to drift into the emotional areas.

16.6   Evaluating customers' business plans

This topic overlaps with practice of banking where it is covered in great detail, although it is of consequence so below are some key points for consideration in evaluating customers' proposals etc.

Whatever the request from a customer it will always involve the analysis of the two key items that concern an organization – Risk and Return. This involves the concept of Regret – what will I regret if I do consent to this proposal. Ie what is the risk to us if we do this? – and equally what will we regret if we do not agree? We might lose the customer or profit.

The key question is 'does the proposal from the customer make sense?' – ie do the numbers stack up and what could go wrong that might alter them.

In general terms customers' plans are optimistic and it is necessary to go right down to the assumptions level and question these until you are comfortable with them.

Some general *aides-mémoire* for this are as follows:

CAMPARI (character, ability, management, purpose, amount, repayment, insurance)

PAPERS (purpose, amount, period, earnings, repayment, security)

(others include CCC and RADAR). These are only acronyms of course and serve only to remind you that you must investigate the points to your satisfaction.

What a plan should contain

In general a plan should set out all salient points, summarized, and a typical structure would be as follows:

- **Summary** – which draws out the key features – including key performance indicators
- **Introduction and description of business** – to set the context and inform as to what the business does. This is useful later on for assessing the plan in the right business environment
- **Market analysis** – the market that they are in – the trends, customer base and profiles etc
- **Internal situation analysis** – their strengths and weaknesses – what they offer and why customers should buy from them etc
- **Marketing plan** – how they intend to persuade their customers to buy their offerings (CVP etc)
- **Operating plan** – how the business will function
- **Financials** – cash flow, revenue expected, profit and loss, balance sheets etc
- **Resource requirements** – plant, machinery, IT systems and people and skills needed
- **Appendices** – useful supporting documentation – extra details

The plan should also contain details of the targets, which may be quantitative or qualitative – eg

- Financial returns
- Costs (absolute and relative)
- Market share (and, if they are on the ball, product penetration by customer)
- Manpower
- Sales/volume of business
- Growth
- Customer satisfaction
- Quality of outputs

The length and depth of the plan may vary – a sole trader will not produce anything like the detail that a plc might – but the core items should be there and have been thought through so that they will stand up to your careful probing.

In looking at any plan there are three things that are key:

- management

- management

- management

without good and capable management then the best plan in the world will not achieve its goals.

Key learning points

1. Dealing with organizations is very different from dealing with individuals.

2. Remember that a presentation is like an iceberg – 90% is unseen (below the waterline) and is in the planning and preparation. The delivery although important is only the tip.

3. Complaints must be dealt with effectively – customer satisfaction increases dramatically after a successful resolution of an error.

4. To make meetings or interviews truly effective you must conduct them properly and ensure that you keep out of the 'emotional' areas.

17

CONTINUING IMPROVEMENT

Topics in this chapter

- Customer feedback

- Performance measures

- Benchmarking – internally, within sector, best in class

Syllabus topics covered

- The importance of effective Customer Relationship Management strategies as an integral part of effective financial services marketing strategies for retail and business customers.

- Customer Relationship Management as part of a customer service quality strategy.

- Customer satisfaction.

Introduction

It is of little value merely implementing a Customer Relationship Management initiative and then sitting back and feeling 'warm'. The world does not stand still and your customers' needs change – as do those of your staff. It is, therefore, important that the foundations for continuing improvement are laid right at the outset.

17.1 Performance measures

If the corporate strategy sets the overall goals and competitive strategy sets them in relation to offerings, it is important to know whether or not you are achieving the goals through your Customer Relationship Management programme and, therefore, delivering value. Thus, to this end some degree of measurement is needed. It is necessary to quantify all goals by setting the targets that must be measured. In the context of Customer Relationship Management of course you need to relate the targets back to the activities that support it.

Figure 68: Key performance indicators – diagrammatically

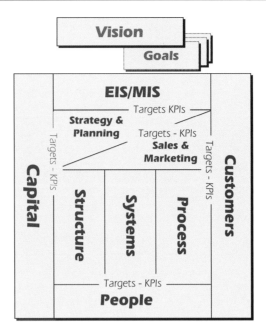

These quantified targets are known as the Key Performance Indicators and must be set for all aspects of the organization to enable you to measure success or not. They are shown diagrammatically above. They must measure all aspects of operations and should focus on these areas:

● measures for **customer** excellence that demonstrate how you are delivering your goods for value;

● measures for **stakeholders** with the principal classes being management, staff and suppliers of capital; and

● internal measures for **excellence** which tell executives how well the organization is performing.

17.2   Measures for customers

Any company that is considered excellent will have a well-established and effective mechanism for measuring how well customers feel that they are serviced. It may consist of several activities but the main point is that these are collated and that something is done about it where appropriate.

One of the key questions is 'What should you measure?' For many firms the only feedback that they receive is of the negative sort when customers complain about errors or poor service.

To improve, however, you not only need to find out where you are failing to delight your customers but you also need to know where you are managing to achieve this (see Kano analysis). You need to make sure that you are focusing on the right issues and, therefore, hitting critical factors for customers rather than what your organization might assume are the right ones.

The items for measurement must be set not from the organizational point of view – but rather from the customers' perspective. How do I feel about my interactions with the organization?

They might include:

● Measures of customer service such as courtesy or promptness in calling back

● Staff knowledge when dealing with customers

● Turnaround in dealing with complaints

But they should also include some tangible measures that customers are satisfied – such as:

● Product penetration

● Product extension into family

● Referrals etc

Ultimately the only true measure of customers' satisfaction is that they place their business with you. What you are trying to do is pre-empt anything that might stop them from doing it and sort it out before it becomes an issue. This is in line with the precepts of Customer Relationship Management.

17.3   Measures for stakeholders

These are often overlooked when considering improvements but are as critical as any other. Typically measures for the shareholders are considered but it is equally as important to measure other stakeholders. These would include staff, regulators and may include others. As discussed, financial services is heavily dependent on people and customer relationship management by its very nature is as well – therefore, people are an important factor in success and their feedback is required as well. Regulation too is important and one of the key benefits from better customer management should be a reduction in complaints about 'inappropriate behaviour' to regulators or ombudsmen (mis-selling etc). This too should be measured because it forms part of the success.

Examples here could be reduction in staff turnover, improvement in staff morale, enhanced product knowledge, very low levels of complaints to the regulator and so on.

17.4 Measures for excellence

Finally you will want to take note of internal measures that demonstrate how well and how effectively you are carrying out your operations. These measures will quantify such things as:

● Increase in customer profitability

● Greater product penetration

● Improvement in conversion of leads to deals

● Increased staff retention (of the right kind)

● Fewer errors

Figure 69: Performance measures – hierarchy

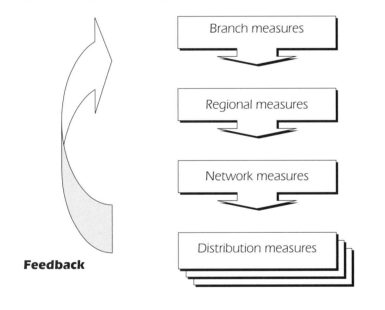

These goals can then be cascaded down to individual levels so that each person can see how they directly contribute to the success of the organization – and of course can then be measured, monitored and managed to further improve things. They can also be aggregated up by channel unit and by channel to provide a detailed analysis of performance.

By setting up performance measures it is then possible to see the benefits from using Customer Relationship Management. Some examples of this include:[27]

---

[27] Aberdeen Group Presentation – Customer Relationship Management – guru 13th November 2001.

Honeywell Industrial Control:

● reduced sales configuration error and after-market sales – US$2m savings

Guaranty Bank:

● Reduced new debit card process by 35% and file time by 50%

● Reduced customer enquiries by 30%

Rockwell Automation

● Decreased order error rate from 70% to 20%

● Stronger ratio of 'quotes to order' from 5:1 to 1.5:1

As these cases demonstrate significant benefits can be gained. In order to understand this, however – and prove it – you need to set your goals in advance and then measure the improvements against them. You then need to take action to rectify deficiencies and obviate errors.

This will feed back into training and thence into new measures and so on, thus creating a virtuous circle on improvement

Key learning points

1. Measurement is critical to improvement.

2. You need to measure all aspects of operations – customers, stakeholders and excellence.

3. You then need to collate the results, analyse them and take action to improve further.

Further reading

Mark Stewart: *Keep the Right Customers* (step 5)

Keaney:

GLOSSARY

Footfall	number of people passing by or through a location
HINWIS	High Net worth Individuals
OLAP	On-Line Analytical Processing
OLTP	On-Line Transaction Processing
CHAPS	Clearing House Automated Patyment System
RDMS	relational database management system
Data Warehouse	method of storing information that facilitates analysis
Data Mining	extracting information from masses of data

FURTHER READING

Change Management Pocketbook	Russell-Jones	Management Pocketbooks
Competitive Advantage	Porter	Free Press
Decision Making Pocketbook	Russell-Jones	Management Pocketbooks
EVA	Stewart	John Wiley
FT – Mastering Marketing	Various	FT
FT – Mastering Strategy	Various	FT
Funky Business	Ridderstrale & Nordstrom	FT.com
Keep the Right Customer	M Stewart	McGraw-Hill
Key Accounts are Different	Langdon	Pitman
Principles of Marketing	Kotler	Prentice Hall
Pyramid Thinking	Barbara Minto	Pitman
Relationship Marketing	Stone & Woodcock	Kogan-Page
Strategic Planning	Ansoff	Penguin
Strategic Safari	Mintzberg	Prentice Hall
Value Pricing	Fletcher & Russell-Jones	Kogan Page
Values in Decision Making	Richard Keaney	Harvard
The Whole Business Brain	Ned Herrmann	McGraw-Hill

INDEX
